PRESERVATION HALL

PRESERVATION HALL

Photographs by
SHANNON BRINKMAN

Interviews with Preservation Hall Band Members by
EVE ABRAMS

Louisiana State University Press
Baton Rouge

Published by Louisiana State University Press
Copyright © 2011 by Louisiana State University Press
Photographs copyright © 2011 by Shannon Brinkman
Manufactured in China
LSU Press Paperback Original
FIRST PRINTING

Designer: AMS
Typeface: Helvetica Neue
Printer and binder: Everbest Printing Co., through Four Colour Imports, Ltd., Louisville, Kentucky

Library of Congress Cataloging-in-Publication Data

Brinkman, Shannon, 1965–
  Preservation Hall / photographs by Shannon Brinkman ; interviews with Preservation Hall Band
members by Eve Abrams.
      p. cm.
  ISBN 978-0-8071-3726-0 (pbk. : alk. paper)
  1. Jazz musicians—Louisiana—New Orleans—Interviews. 2. Jazz musicians—Louisiana—New
Orleans—Portraits. 3. Jazz—Louisiana—New Orleans—Pictorial works. 4. Preservation Hall Jazz
Band—Pictorial works. I. Abrams, Eve, 1971– II. Title.
  ML3508.8.N48B75 2011
  781.6509763'35—dc22
                                                                                          2010037994

The paper in this book meets the guidelines for permanence and durability of the Committee on
Production Guidelines for Book Longevity of the Council on Library Resources. ∞

To John Brunious, Walter Payton, Ralph Johnson,
Ernest "Doc" Watson, and Anthony "Tuba Fats" Lacen

I sing because I'm happy,
I sing because I'm free,
For His eye is on the sparrow,
And I know He watches me.
—gospel hymn by Civilla D. Martin and Charles H. Gabriel

Looking forward to meeting you all again one day . . .

Contents

Foreword

All of us who were present in the early days knew that Preservation Hall was a special place. We had a sense that the Hall was more than a musical venue; it was an important force for reviving traditional jazz—not just the music as an art form, but the lives and culture of the musicians themselves. A lot of the older musicians had quit playing. Allan Jaffe went around town on his Vespa, and every time he would hear about a musician who wasn't playing anymore, he would try to get them on their feet and working at the Hall. It was almost like a religious revival—a phoenix-like resurrection from the ashes. It was a sense that we are blowing on the embers of something that was dying and now may no longer be dying. We can help it live again.

Apart from that revival aspect, there was the infectious joy and warmth and humanity of the musicians that really communicated at a time when whites and blacks could not socialize legally. The Hall was a place where we did share something. First of all, the music. But we would also talk and laugh together and get to know each other. We would visit the musicians in their homes, and they would visit us. We felt a great sense of curiosity about these people, the way they lived, their neighborhoods, the way they talked, the way they made a living, the way they dressed. It wasn't a completely foreign culture, but it was very different from what I had grown up with in my white middle-class world. We were reaching out over all these age barriers and race and economic barriers and class barriers, and just coming together on the basis of our common humanity.

Those experiences made the Hall something very special, and everybody who came down there regularly, I think, felt that we belonged to a big family—almost a movement, a cause. That was very important to us, even if we didn't articulate it in those terms. I think everybody sensed that this was not just a club where you went to hear music. It was much, much more than that.

Tom Sancton

Acknowledgments

I want to thank Benji Jaffe for believing in me, for asking me to make an art book about Preservation Hall, and for letting me take eight years to do it.

Thanks to all the wonderful people who work at Preservation Hall in the present and the past. A special, huge thanks to Debbie Guidry, Resa Lambert, Kate Fogle, and Howard Lambert for all your help and for letting me in the door.

Thank you to Roy DeCarava, the now-deceased author and photographer of *The Sound I Saw,* which lent me confidence in my vision for the book.

Thank you, Bryce Lankard, for helping me edit the images initially and for giving me my first partner to work with.

Thank you to my parents for always asking me, "When is this going to be done?"

Thank you, Eve Abrams, for asking questions that always surprised me and for making this book a reality.

Most of all, I want to say thank you to all the musicians who make the Hall what it is. Every last one of you—living and not living. Thank you for continuously inspiring me and educating me on New Orleans jazz and life. Thank you for your music—for making me cry and laugh at the same time. Without this project, I wouldn't be who I am today.

For the New Orleans jazz community and to help ensure its future, part of my proceeds from the sale of this book will go to the Preservation Hall Junior Jazz and Heritage Brass Band.

Shannon Brinkman

Thanks to all the musicians who answered my many, many questions and shared their stories with me. I feel honored.

Some of the oral interviews in this book have been slightly adjusted for the written format.

Eve Abrams

PRESERVATION HALL

RICKIE MONIE: The Hall is a New Orleans treasure. We have people that come from all over the world to Preservation Hall. I've seen the line wrap around the corner just to get into the Hall and listen at the music.

Introduction

My parents spent six weeks in Mexico for their honeymoon and came through New Orleans on their way back to Philadelphia, where my father had a job waiting for him at a department store. While here, they happened on a parade one day—a demonstration of a funeral procession being conducted by the Tulane Jazz Archives. They followed the parade back to Preservation Hall—only at the time, it wasn't called Preservation Hall. It was an art gallery called Consolidated Artists, or 726 St. Peter Street, named after the address. The owner of the gallery, Larry Borenstein, had jam sessions over here. During the week, he invited musicians over to play—he called them rehearsals—and they would pass a kitty around for tips. Larry discovered that by having music here, more people would come in and look at the artwork. Some people started coming only for the music.

My parents—Allan and Sandra Jaffe—ended up getting an apartment on Royal Street. My father worked at D. H. Holmes department store on Canal Street during the day and here, at Preservation Hall, at night. At first it was donation only. It was day by day: let's just do this and see what happens, with no real long-term business plan. It evolved into them having sessions on a regular basis. They started going into neighborhoods to track down musicians who were still performing this kind of music but not making it into the French Quarter.

At that time, jazz in general wasn't being performed like it is today. In the 1960s in New Orleans, there were no jazz clubs. There were bars or burlesque shows that had a jazz accompaniment, and there may have been places on Bourbon Street that had more Dixieland-style music, but not dignified jazz like what's going on here at Preservation Hall. Here, there are no distractions from the music. It's funny; I saw this interview of my dad early on in 1961, and he says, "We're not trying to hustle drinks and there are no strippers." That was a real selling point! To be in the French Quarter and doing that was very progressive at the time. And to be featuring African American musicians with a predominantly white audience was unheard of. A venue dedicated to jazz made the statement that this music had artistic validity and cultural significance. This was pre–civil rights movement. It was still the Jim Crow South.

Larry Borenstein was an interesting person. He was part art dealer, music lover, importer, property owner . . . an all-around French Quarter character. Larry recognized something unique in my parents. My dad graduated from the Wharton School of Business, but he also had a military background. He had a different perspective than others—a special, higher regard for the arts and culture.

My parents dove into the deep end quickly. They were involved in creating the Society for the Preservation of New Orleans Jazz—that's where the name Preservation Hall comes from. They made a pact between themselves that they were going to remain in New Orleans until the civil rights laws were passed, and then they would return to Philadelphia. But as most of us know who are lifers here, once its roots are in you, there's no leaving. You can leave, but then you're always missing it.

In 1963, my parents brought the first Preservation Hall band to perform in Minneapolis, and in 1964 they returned to perform at the Guthrie Theater. That show resulted in Sweet Emma Barrett and Her Preservation Hall Jazz Band—the first recording by a Preservation Hall band. My parents never moved back to Philadelphia. They took over the lease from Larry, and the Preservation Hall Band went on to tour the world.

I remember when the lease came up in 1985. My dad sat us all down at the kitchen table and asked us what we should do. My parents felt they had accomplished their mission: they created an institution, and it lived its life. Many of the musicians that played here in the early days—Punch Miller, Sweet Emma Barrett, George Lewis, the people who were the bedrock of Preservation Hall—were gone. They had passed away, and now we were into the next generation of New Orleans jazz musicians. Albeit, these guys were still in their seventies and eighties, but it was different. It wasn't that first wave of musicians my parents first met when they arrived in New Orleans. So there was a real dilemma of whether or not to continue. The mission of Preservation Hall— to perpetuate the New Orleans music tradition and to provide work for living musicians who created this style of music—had evolved. By the 1980s, the musicians playing at the Hall were second- and third-generation New Orleans jazz musicians, and the style of music had also evolved as time passed and the Hall grew in popularity.

I was thirteen, and my dad asked me: What do you think I should do? I didn't understand the dilemma. To me, the Preservation Hall that existed during my lifetime was the only one I knew. I said, Well, of course you continue it; you don't close it. Then we had a little conversation about whether this was something I would want to continue when I was older. So in the back of my mind was the idea that this is where I would end up. But it wasn't something I thought about as a teenager. I was probably more serious than most of the kids my age, and I was involved in the music scene, but to consciously think I'm going to take over Preservation Hall? No. But an opportunity presented itself.

My father passed away in 1987 when I was sixteen. The bass player who took over his chair, James Prevost, took me under his wing and let me practice on his bass while touring. I carried it for him, and tuned it for him before the shows, and set up his microphone. Mr. Prevost was aging and didn't want to tour as frequently. So literally the day after I graduated college in 1993, I flew off to meet the band in France and immediately became the bass player with the band and oversaw the operations of Preservation Hall from the road. I was twenty-two.

I think Preservation Hall was instrumental in ensuring the future of our musical traditions. Something my father instilled in me was the concept that New Orleans music managed to exist all of these years because it was financially rewarding to the musicians. It served not only a social function; it was also a job. These guys woke up, ironed their shirts, put on their suits, and went to work. Preservation Hall served an incredible role in making sure there were brass bands, and there were funerals happening, and there was music at events. I think we changed the direction of history in certain ways. Without Preservation Hall, there wouldn't be the current generation of musicians. A lot of guys will attest to that.

But we're not just here to preserve New Orleans music. We're here to perpetuate cultural traditions and embrace the artistic spirit of New Orleans. Preservation Hall is just one little piece of the cultural pie. A big part of my mission is to expose new audiences to our music and to ensure certain cultural traditions continue: that there are churches, that there are music programs, that there are second-line parades, that there are Mardi Gras Indians, that there are social aid and pleasure clubs, that there are benevolent associations, that there are Mardi Gras krewes, that the Zulus are here. All of those things are extremely important to this fragile ecosystem. You remove one thing—we lose one musician—and there's a domino effect.

There are musicians who play different styles of music who I've encouraged to take an interest in New Orleans Jazz and Preservation Hall. I'm following in the spirit of my dad—the way he made sure younger musicians had instruments, or pulled them off the street to listen to the band at the Hall. That encouragement goes a long way when you're a younger musician. You see, contemporary and modern exist in New Orleans, but at the same time, it's also very old. When you use the word "traditional" you immediately pigeonhole the music as something that happened in the past, and that bothers me. No. It's still happening today! I call what we play at Preservation Hall "New Orleans jazz" or "New Orleans music." What did they call it before it was called jazz? It's "traditional New Orleans jazz." It's "contemporary traditional New Orleans jazz"!

Anybody—any artist or person who experiences Preservation Hall—immediately knows that there is something very, very special here. That it's extremely unique.

That's what I find amazing about Preservation Hall: somehow, the right people always find it.

Ben Jaffe

WALTER PAYTON: A tradition has to have an institution to perpetuate it. Whether it's an institution that teaches or whether it's an institution that allows the tradition to survive or to thrive—it needs a place to be nurtured, and that's Preservation Hall.

CHARLIE GABRIEL: Music is spiritual. When it touches you it does something to you, and you does something to the music. Music lasts and it breathes. Once it gets into the environment, it never dies. It keeps moving and everybody that touches it does something to it and it does something to them. Music is colorless and it's a spirit within one another. Some of us is blessed to nurse that spirit that we have, that God-given gift.

TOM SANCTON: The first time I heard George Lewis play—the sound of his horn—just that tone was angelic. I just thought it was pure distilled beauty and passion and love and I couldn't even find words for it, but it's something that attracted me almost like a siren's song.

JOHN BRUNIOUS: It's just a great feeling, knowing that people are just wondering what's gonna come out of your horn.

MICHAEL PIERCE: Music is emotions. That goes hand in hand.

LUCIEN BARBARIN: The trombone is the slide instrument. It shouldn't be played fast. I dance with it. I try to paint a picture with it. I try to get the people to feel the emotions what I'm feeling, what I'm thinking about during the time. If it's anger, you'll hear that anger in sound. If it's sweetness—if I'm thinking of pleasant stuff—you'll hear the pleasant, you'll hear the quietness, you'll hear the peaceful sound.

MARK BRAUD: When you go there—when you walk through that door—and you see all the people there that are waiting for you to perform, it's a good feeling. Because you know that the music is still alive, still a treasure.

CLIVE WILSON: The records tell you what the music is but it doesn't tell you why. When you see it live in a function, you see why they're playing that tempo—because people are dancing, or you see what they're really feeling when they play that way, if it's blues or something. When you hear a record you have to imagine everything, and you're not going to imagine everything exactly.

BEN JAFFE: I definitely feel like it's a protected place. I revere this space the way one would a church—a church in New Orleans—which has its doors open and welcomes people to be there.

DANIEL FARROW: You got to really feel it to play it. Every note connects. Just like speaking. Your fingers, they do it by themselves, you can't stop them. And that's the best way to play: natural. 'Cause you don't know what you're going to play until you start playing. You just feel it in your body.

GREGG STAFFORD: When I walk on stage, I'm standing on the shoulders of a lot of great men that I had the opportunity to share my life with. They live in me. That's what you feel coming through my instrument—all those old guys. I shared time with them, ate with them, sweated with them. That's what comes through the horn.

LUCIEN BARBARIN: My ancestors also played traditional jazz. So now I'm keeping the tradition alive and carrying on my ancestors' legacy. Maybe one day I'll be up on one of these pictures that's on the walls of Preservation Hall. And maybe they'll say, "Hey, remember that guy there . . ."

WILL SMITH: I grew up right in this very place. If you look back there in that room there's what used to be a bathroom for the musicians. I scribbled my name on the wall there in '72. I was ten years old then. So, I've been around here my whole life.

CARL LEBLANC: The note A vibrates 440 times a second, and that's what makes A. 880 is the next A. Each light in the spectrum also has a vibration per second, and so there's a color that matches each sound. Some people see them. Children do.

MICHAEL PIERCE: I looked at traditional music as an old tradition, and I wanted to venture off it because I'd just come from New York, and I was into that avant garde. When I came back to New Orleans, I had to relearn real tradition. I found out that you have to go back to go forward.

DARRYL ADAMS: I started playing when I was six years old. My mother taught me. I always wanted to switch to drums, but my mama wouldn't let me.

JOHN BRUNIOUS: At the Hall, you have a rapport with the audience, and to me, that makes the music more interesting, with the people right up on you. I could touch them with my big toe.

CARL LEBLANC: In New Orleans you have music for everything. Like in the culture as a whole, you have music for Happy Birthday. There's a song for that. There's a song for Here Come the Bride. There's a song for specific occasions. I understand in Africa there's a song when the sun rises. There's a song when it's time to get the harvest. In Africa, where music was such an integral part of life, there wasn't even a word for music, because it wasn't separate. It was just part of everything that went on. So, meet somewhere in the middle, and you find New Orleans.

MAYNARD CHATTERS: When we think of jazz and how it started, the brass bands are really your first bands. The inception of New Orleans jazz started back around 1890, 1900. Tuxedo, The Olympia, Onward Brass Band: all those bands that started back around that time. I heard that music all my life, for the funerals and all the social events. Bands played up and down the streets. This was a normal thing in New Orleans.

FREDDIE LONZO: I always liked music. I used to follow the parades as far as I thought I could go because I knew my mom was watching me. It might be three or four blocks, but I knew she was watching me. You know: long eyes, long arms of your mother.

MARI WATANABE: The first time I went to a jazz funeral it was—I would say—sight-seeing. The second time and the third time, it was a funeral for somebody I know. Then it was the funeral for friends. One day, it will be my funeral. I hope people come to parade for me.

WILL SMITH: The trumpet is out front. It's the lead. You know, most times when you remember a song you remember the melody. You don't really remember all the other things that go on around it that much. But the melody is the main part of the song. That's part of my reasoning for wanting to play trumpet.

SHANNON POWELL: I had my first drum set at nine. I was beating on the pots and pans at home and all over the furniture. My mother got tired of that. I was destroying the furniture and bending up all the strainers. I was using the strainers for tom-toms. Each pot was made for something—the snare drum, you know. I had dents in them. And every time she go to cook she had to be hitting them, knocking them into shape to cook. The poor strainer caught hell. But it had a good sound.

TOM SANCTON: Sometimes when I'm playing there, I feel like it's a very improbable role for me to be in. You know: what am I doing here? I'm supposed to be on the bench listening to the old guys. Well, the old guys aren't there anymore, and so now, we are the mens.

ERNIE ELLY: My brother, he really had the talent, and he'd be around the house tapping on the radio. On Saturdays we used to do our ironing, and so he'd be listening to jazz, and he'd get a brush and start playing on the radio and stuff. And then I'd try it, and he'd say, "No, no. Listen to it." And so, I really learned from him. He was really my first instructor. But, he never set behind a set.

DOC WATSON: My thing has always been to paint a pretty picture. To paint a pretty picture with song. Always something of beauty. Something you can look out and see the audience really like. Something that they connect with. Now, they like technical stuff, but they recognize a melody; you can see it come over their face, you know.

JOHN ROYEN: It was a whole different education just sitting on a tour bus and listening to these guys recounting stories from their childhood and growing up and playing in New Orleans and in the South. And of course, they came up in the era of segregation and everything else. There was no way I could relate to it as a young white boy from Washington, D.C., but as a young white boy with an education, I knew enough to be quiet and listen and learn and try to understand the values of some of these guys, and also the value that music took in their lives. . . .

   I never once felt like I was an outsider with the old-timers. Not once. And that was just a delightful thing to feel the warmth of all of that. I mean, when you're on a bandstand, and you're playing with guys who have played—even the simplest of tunes—for sixty years, seventy years, and I'm just fitting in right with them and they're totally comfortable with it, and we're all feeding off each other— that transcends seventy years of living in New Orleans when you can sit down and communicate with each other on a musical level. It was a family, and they gave me the honor of letting me be part of the family. I was an adopted son.

LEROY JONES: When all the ingredients of great music are there, it's a natural high—physically and spiritually. And when that happens, the people who are listening in the audience, they feel that. It's infectious. It's like being in church. Music is so powerful it lifts the people up, and when they are lifted up, you are lifted up. They give you something back. You give them something, and they give you something back. It doesn't have to be perfect note for note, but the feeling—if there's love in it, that is the most important thing above all.

WALTER PAYTON: New Orleans jazz needs Preservation Hall, and it needs other halls too. But that's the fountainhead. That's the mountaintop. Preservation Hall is—to New Orleans—what Carnegie Hall is to New York.

ERNIE ELLY: I started taking up drums fifty-two years ago. So, I wouldn't call that playing, but that's when I started.

LUCIEN BARBARIN: In grade school I just so happened to pick up a brass instrument, and I automatically started blowing it. The horn was bigger than I was.

WALTER PAYTON: The instrument and the musician becomes one. It's a marriage that happens. And then it goes out to the rest of the band.

DANIEL FARROW: I touch a lot of people. Some kind of spirit, I guess.

RALPH JOHNSON: When you're playing, you don't feel no sickness. You don't feel no nothing. Everything feels great, it's like a therapy.
    People is the same. If they love the beat and they go to dancing, they doing that 'cause they
happy. It's helping them. I mean people be suffering in this world. Do you know that? Some people
get sick, some get cancer, all kind of sickness. But they hear the music and they forget about that
for that second.

GREGG STAFFORD: I wanted to take music, but growing up as a kid, my mother told me no, I'm not going to buy you an instrument. When I was choosing electives in high school, the music instructor said: grit your teeth; show me your teeth. He said: yes, you take instrumental music. I'll give you a school horn. I was in the right place at the right time according to God's will. The more the years moved along, the more that feeling became prevalent.

WALTER PAYTON: I was like most youngsters: oblivious. Not even realizing the ramifications and the depth of the history of the music that I was being thrown into. But now I can really, really appreciate it.

LEROY JONES: We're trying to play music together, and music is very intimate as you know. It's almost a love affair up there on the stage, and if everything is not right, and feelings and emotions are not right between the musicians, you're going to have a little bit of a problem. It's like a marriage, you know. In music, there has to be musical communication.

RICKIE MONIE: My father was a pianist. He didn't play professionally but he played in church from time to time. Then I'd go down to Preservation Hall and I'd hear the greats, you know, like Sweet Emma, Sing Miller, and Sadie Goodson. So I've been influenced by many different musicians, and I try to take a bit of that and incorporate it in the way I feel. But I didn't want to play like Sweet Emma; I didn't want to play like them. I wanted to develop a style of my own just as they did.

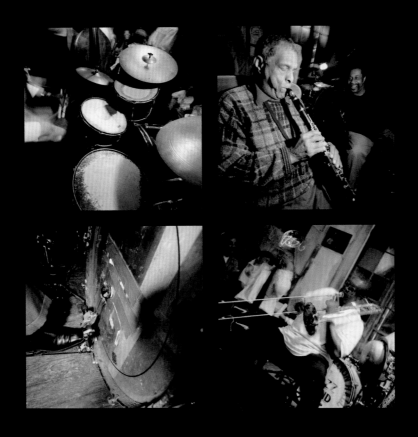

CHARLIE GABRIEL: New Orleans is a very, very, very special place. New Orleans is a place we nurse this music. This music was nursed here and sent out to the universe. If they wouldn't have closed down Storyville in 1917, the music would have stayed right here in New Orleans, but they closed down Storyville and the music went on the boats and went up to New York, went up to Chicago, went to California.

LUCIEN BARBARIN: Once when Willie and Percy [Humphrey] was living—this was back in the early '90s—the Hall asked me to play and I said, "Well, who's in the band?" and they said, "Oh, Willie and Percy." These guys was way older; they was in their nineties then, and I said, "Aw shucks, I don't want to play with them old men." But it dawned on me that, you know what? I'm making a foolish choice here. I can actually learn something from these older guys. And when I came that particular day and I sat there and I looked at these guys and I listened to them, I said to myself: "Wow, how stupid was I?" You have to follow under the footsteps of the greats that went before you.

MAYNARD CHATTERS: This was the thing with New Orleans jazz, or traditional jazz. It's freedom. It gives you that sense of freedom. We say that jazz is American music, which it is. It's the only true American music because we think of opera, you know, we think of symphonic music—that's all European music. That music did not develop in the United States of America. The only true music that really developed in America is jazz. That is American.

JOHN "KID" SIMMONS: The musicians we were trying to emulate came up without radio or TV. Whatever they heard, they heard live. Now the musicians playing this style came up playing modern jazz, rhythm and blues, listening to whatever on the radio. All of that comes through in their interpretation of the music.

DANIEL FARROW: I think a lot of old musicians who passed away—I feel them. I feel the love in them. I produce that in my music. Guys I heard play, and some things they played, I can just feel it. It comes out in my sound, in my music. You tell a story. It's a story in your mind.

KERRY HUNTER: They have some cats that could read music, and they have some cats that can't read music. But if you pay attention, the cat that can't read music—he's giving the cat that can read music a little bit of trouble over here on that trombone or that trumpet. So, it's really—it's like a feel for the music. If you're not playing it with a feeling, it's not going to really show you the spirit of the person who's playing. They got it written down, songs in the traditional way, how it was—but you listen to that, how that played compared to a person playing it the way they feel it—and it's two different sounds.

BEN JAFFE: If Preservation Hall were in New York, people would have figured it out. This represents this. That's not so easy in New Orleans. Tuba Fats is a great example. Played tuba with the Olympia Brass Band, masked as a Mardi Gras Indian, was an original member of the Sixth Ward Dirty Dozen Band. Went to church and learned gospel. He didn't just go to school and learn one thing. He picked up a little bit here, a little bit there.

BEN JAFFE: The name "Preservation" is something I've always battled with because the way that's used in other artistic contexts means this is something that's existed; we've defined what it is, and that's what it will always be. That's not New Orleans music. The funeral traditions are a great example of the way something is exactly what it was one hundred years ago, socially. Musically, it's evolved, but the tradition itself, at its root, is still the same. Having music there gives us the opportunity to mourn and then also to celebrate the deceased's memory. The music's a little different now, the songs are a little different. The bands don't necessarily wear shirts and ties and marching caps anymore, but at its root, the function of the event is exactly the same. That's the reason I have trouble with the word "preservation" and the way that it's used to describe what we do because people think we're recreating something which happened a hundred years ago, and I have to come back and explain: no, this is a really live music in a cultural tradition that still exists today.

WILL SMITH: The music's got to evolve. We're not the same people. We didn't hear some of the stuff that the first generation heard that influenced the music up until the '70s—to when I started listening to it and being a student of it. So, we don't have those same influences, but we do have the influence of what they've done, and it's sort of evolved. I think the '70s was a huge turning point for the music.

   The sort of style you hear playing very commonly now has become like swing trad. It's like it's taken a more swingy kind of feel over the years, and that's absolutely not a bad thing, but I think it has a lot to do with how it's perceived rhythmically. That's from so many people not being exposed to it over part of its life span—so you get people who were trained classically or were trained in blues or some other form of jazz, and then they come here and wind up playing this style. So it's sort of meshing with a lot of other things that have helped it sort of morph.

MARK BRAUD: It's a great honor to play at Preservation Hall because so many great giants of music have come through Preservation Hall. To walk in those footsteps is pretty huge for a young person like me. To listen to this music all my life, and now, I'm getting to play with some of the musicians that I grew up listening to. So it's an honor to play in the band because of the ones who came before. And the ones who are in the band now—it's a great pleasure and honor to play with them too.

THADDEUS RICHARD: It's easier to play music and entertain someone if you have them already laughing. It opens the door. It's entertainment. It's not just music. A lot of jazz guys take themselves so serious. I'm here to entertain people using whatever skills I have.

LEROY JONES: By the late '70s, we were already beginning to innovate the brass band sound through different bass lines that Tuba Fats was laying out, and different riffs we were creating in the trumpet section. But the foundation is still within that tradition. If you were to lay down that same groove against what they're doing today, you can hear the correlation between the two. It's not that different. We were doing it the way we experienced in our day. If we'd grown up in the 1920s, where there was no other music being played on the radio that would have influenced our process of playing, then we would have played it the way the old Eureka, the old Onward, the old Tuxedo, the old Olympia Brass Band played it.

DARRYL ADAMS: If I don't make someone cry—to be straight-up honest with you—I haven't done my job. If I don't make you try to reach the sky, I haven't done my job.

JOHN BRUNIOUS: Musicians call their lips their chops. God had blessed me with a great pair of chops that I was able to play high notes.

CHARLIE GABRIEL: I went up to Detroit in 1948, and every year my dad brought me back to New Orleans. I used to get so angry about my father bringing me back to New Orleans every year. I used to say, "Dad, man," I say, "they got good musicians all over the world, ain't only good musicians in New Orleans." He would say, "Boy, you're wet behind the ear. You've got a wooden ear." I realized what he was trying to tell me—there are *special* musicians here in New Orleans. They got so much feeling in the music.

DARRYL ADAMS: If you never play a second line in the street, you will never understand this music. You might think you do, but you don't. You've never experienced the joy and the happiness if you've never experienced the funerals.

DANIEL FARROW: I just be happy. I've been like that all my life. Good times, bad times, always happy.

WALTER PAYTON: Some people don't know the difference between the sousaphone and the tuba. It sits in your lap. You don't wear it; you bare it. The bass you have to wrap yourself around and cuddle it.

CLINT MAEDGEN: I sing 'cause it makes me feel alive. It's been a tremendous opportunity for me to kind of stretch my wings and sing in different styles and actually sing, like that whole jazz singer kind of thing where you're sounding pretty and you have control.

It's time-traveling, really. I mean it could be 1961, or '73 or '84 or anything else because that room hasn't changed at all. Any chance I get to perform there . . . I just jump at it. I want to spend the rest of my life with Preservation Hall. I'm really hoping that can work.

RALPH JOHNSON: It's like going to a beautiful place in sound.

JOHN BRUNIOUS: We get people from every country, and they enjoy the music so much that it really transcends. No matter where you're from, music is a universal language. They may not understand what you're saying verbally, but musically, they feel what you're doing.

"LITTLE JOE" LASTIE: Playing in the Hall has the same spiritual feeling that I get when I was playing in the church. I learned how to play in the church. Because my grandfathers, they the first ones that I seen playing drums in the church. And they used to play that press roll. Same thing that I play at Preservation Hall. When they used to do it, the spirit was so much there, you get that shaking. I get that same shake when I play with Preservation Hall. I get that movement.

CARL LEBLANC: Music is medicinal. And it also is a direct contact to the spirit. I went to an old folks' home and was playing for this man with no legs—an older man. I started playing "Sweet Lorraine," and he started crying. I mean, not tears, I mean boo-hooing—wailing. And I say, "What's the matter, man?" He say, "That was me and my wife's song. We were married for 50–60 years, and every time we heard it we danced." And, he's crying. I say, "You want me to stop?" He say, "No." And, the whole while I played it he just balled like a baby.

FREDDIE LONZO: The horn is probably my crutch. I'm pretty happy when I have the horn in my hand because it's something I can kind of control. It kind of does what I want it to do. Not that I am a control freak, no. It's pleasurable. I'm comfortable with the horn. I'm scrambling for words right now, but if I had my horn I'd be a little better off.

TOM SANCTON: Those chairs are pretty old in there, you know, and the room looks exactly the same, but it's when I'm not playing—when I'm alone in that room—that I feel the ghosts. I see their portraits on the wall, and I kind of still hear the notes echoing in my memory. And sometimes, when I'm alone back in the courtyard where they used to have a lot of parties and jam sessions at night, I feel like I can almost see them back there. I'm very much aware of their presence, and that's not a burden. But it is a sense of belonging to a chain, to having my place in a chain of experience and culture, and it's humbling but also very gratifying, and I feel very privileged to be in this position.

DIMITRI SMITH: The sousaphone is the bottom. It's part of the rhythm section—part of the drums and the bass. We keep the time. If we lose time, the front line lose time. Each instrument holds its own—from lead trumpet to clarinet to trombone tailgating—but the tuba is setting the bottom, setting where the time is gonna go. You put all that together, it's like making a pot of gumbo, really.

CLIVE WILSON: Harold Dejan, who was the leader of the Olympia Brass Band, said come and bring your horn we're going to parade on Sunday. It's all day. Jolly bunch parade. It was eight hours. In August. Very hot. I jumped at the chance. I played with the band all the way. And then [Kid] Sheik said: you're the first white guy to play the whole parade. And the reason was I'd just arrived at the right time. The Civil Rights Act had just been passed in July1964, if I remember correctly. This was August. So segregation was finished, at least officially.

TRADITIONAL Request 2.00
— OTHERS $5.00
The SAINTS $10.00

PRESERVATION

JAZZ
BAND
of
New Orleans

RALPH JOHNSON: I've had people come up to me and say: Mister, you don't know what you did for me. And that means something to me when you hear that. I tell them thank you because that's my goal. Why not do something, you know? Something real, something alive, something good.

WILL SMITH: The older musicians were just majestic. I mean, they wore suits a lot. Almost all of them, to a one, wore these Stacy Adams shoes which they kept shined. I remember once . . . I stepped on Willie Humphrey's shoe right there. And, I mean, I was a kid, and he grabbed me by the arm; he said, "Boy, watch it! Don't ever do that again. That's Stacy Adams." They were just great human beings and characters—extreme characters, actually. They were very distinguished gentle-men. Very distinguished, and very nice.

DARRYL ADAMS: I'm a traditional guy. I'm going to wear black pants, white shirt till the day that I die.

KATJA TOIVOLA: There's been women working at the Hall—there have been piano and banjo players—but as far as I know, I'm the first horn player to work there. If somebody had told me ten years ago that I would actually be playing at the Hall, I would have laughed really hard. Life has mysterious ways. The people that played there—Jim Robinson, Mr. Nelson, and Frog—those were the people I listened to constantly fifteen years ago, and to think that I'm actually sitting in the seat that they were sitting in so many times . . . The first gigs I played at the Hall, I was so nervous my knees were shaking.

LARS EDEGRAN: The first day I was in New Orleans I came to Preservation Hall. I came by in the afternoon and they were having a rehearsal in here for a recording session. Allan Jaffe, the founder of Preservation Hall, was here, and I got invited in by him, which I thought was amazing. I was standing right by the gate here, and he was inside, and I hear the music and I'm peeping in—because I didn't even know what this place looked like or anything. So he asked me if I was interested in music and I said yes; I'm a musician. I played in Sweden before I came over here. I told him a little bit about my story, and that's when he invited me in. And then he let me sit in and play a song with the band—which I thought was really amazingly friendly for somebody to talk to a new person in town, who had no credits whatsoever. But anyway, that was my first experience in Preservation Hall.

WILL SMITH: I love this music. I love it. I mean, it's the most important thing that I've found in life. If I had an argument with you, I'd go play a gig. When I come back—you'd say, "I said what?" I mean, it's totally spiritual; it's extreme therapy. It takes me away from everything. It's one of the best things I've found in life.

MARI WATANABE: If I chose to play music in Japan, I have to give up sooner or later. That's just a temporary thing. But here I saw old people playing music all of their life. I guess I thought if I come here, I can play music till I die, and that's the only thing I really thought about. When I came to New Orleans and saw old musicians playing, I said, well maybe I just play music here and stay here.

SHANNON POWELL: I add everything into the music. When I'm playing I don't hold back nothing. I play the way I feel. And the result is that the music is always growing. It may sound different, but I always make it sound like it's part of the traditional music.

THADDEUS RICHARD: The style we play here is funkier, if you can relate that to jazz. It's a total experience. It's an intellectual reality. It's something that you feel and that you know, but it is hard to put into words.

We're all striving to create magic. That's the ultimate goal.

MITCHELL PLAYER: What artists do a lot, when they're starting, you go: well, I like the way this musician plays so we'll listen and practice and try to sound like them. And then you say, well, I like the way that musician plays, and you listen, and you practice, and you try to sound like them. You go through this period where you're like really checking out all these different artists and what you really like, and a lot of us never really get past that. But in the old days, there were artists who went past that, and then created their own individual thing. That's what made the music so very special.

MAYNARD CHATTERS: Instruments are nothing but extensions of the human voice. God gave all of us a natural instrument, the voice. That is the greatest instrument of all, the human voice.

BEN JAFFE: For me, what the Hall represents is the creative community of New Orleans. It represents the food of New Orleans, it represents the art of New Orleans, it represents the lifestyle of New Orleans. You know, it's much more than just music. This is what's really hard to explain to people.

CHARLIE GABRIEL: When I close my eyes, I'd like to close my eyes in New Orleans.

The Players

Compiled by Eve Abrams and Ben Jaffe with substantial assistance from the musicians, their fans, and their families

DARRYL ADAMS

Alto saxophonist Darryl "Little Jazz" Adams started playing music when he was six years old. Darryl played in concert and symphony bands in school as well as rock and roll combos on the weekends. In those days, every corner in New Orleans had a barroom or a hall with live music, and Darryl played in similar venues outside of town starting when he was around ten years old. He played rhythm and blues in a combo band that opened for the Meters, the Fabulous Phantoms, and many more. Darryl came up under Danny Barker as a member of the Fairview Baptist Church Band, as well as Harold Dejan, the head of the Olympia Brass Band (and also an alto saxophone player!), who took Darryl under his wing when he was sixteen. Darryl spent two months in 1975 putting together "Blackbird Special"—a song fusing jazz, traditional music, funk, and the brass band beat—but the result was the beginning of a new sound popular with younger generations of brass band fans. Darryl also wrote "Tornado Special" and 'Hot Dog Man." Darryl is a lover of tradition and the leader of the Tornado Brass Band. He says when you're in a second line, you have to watch the people. If you're just playing, you'll never learn. He says playing "is almost like runner's high. It's like being in the church in the choir and you sung it so good tears start running down."

Ben Jaffe: Darryl grew up like me, always around music. Following behind parades, sneaking into music clubs. I remember Darryl telling me the story of how he got in the Olympia Band: "I was sixteen. I was outside cutting the grass and your godfather [Harold Dejan] came by the house in his Lincoln Continental. He went inside to talk to my mother. After a while, he came back out, got in his car, and drove off. My mother came out and told me,

'From now on, you're in the Olympia. Leave all them others alone.' And that's how I got started."

LUCIEN BARBARIN

For five generations, the Barbarin family has been integral to the music of New Orleans. Isidore Barbarin mentored the young Louis Armstrong nearly a century ago, and years later, Armstrong recruited Isidore's son Paul to play drums with his band. Today, the torch rests in the hands of trombonist Lucien Barbarin, who made his musical debut at age six, playing drums with his Uncle Paul's Onward Brass Band. In grade school, Lucien picked up a baritone horn and automatically started making sense out of it. His teacher took notice and asked if he wanted to play the horn, but Lucien replied, "I don't know, I gotta ask my parents first." Though his mother said yes, when Lucien arrived home with a suitcase bigger than he was, she was a little skeptical. In junior high school, when there weren't enough tuba players in the band, Lucien volunteered to play that horn too! By high school, Lucien was focusing on trombone. He went on to play rhythm and blues gigs around New Orleans with the groups Stone Mountain and Joy, but an invitation to work with drummer Albert "June" Gardner drew Lucien toward traditional jazz. Since then, Lucien has played with the Tuxedo Brass Band, Wynton Marsalis, Dianne Reeves, Doc Cheatham, and Lionel Hampton. Lucien began bringing his lyrical and sometimes humorous presence to Preservation Hall's stage in the early 1980s. Lucien draws the crowd in with his energy and charm, and then dazzles them with his horn work. When he's not touring, Lucien helps raise his five children, one of whom is named for Lucien's beloved Uncle Paul. Call it fate, destiny, or just coincidence, but Paul plays the drums.

DAVE BARTHOLOMEW

To many of the musicians who regularly play at Preservation Hall, Dave Bartholomew is simply "The Force." A songwriter, producer, arranger, bandleader, and horn player whose musical career spans over seventy years and almost as many musical genres—from rhythm and blues to big band to rock-and-roll to jazz—Dave began blowing music through a tuba and later switched to trumpet. Born upriver from New Orleans in Edgard, Louisiana, Dave took to the water at nineteen when he began playing with the Fats Pichon band aboard the riverboat SS *Capitol.* During World War II, Dave played in the U.S. Army band, and shortly thereafter he began collaborating with Antoine "Fats" Domino, with whom he produced and co-wrote a bounty of record hits, including "The Fat Man," "Ain't It a Shame," "Blueberry Hill," and "Blue Monday." But the hits go on! Dave produced and co-wrote songs with Lloyd Price, Smiley Lewis, Shirley and Lee, and Earl King. Dave's songs have been recorded by scores of artists, including Elvis Presley, Pat Boone, Elton John, the Rolling Stones, Paul McCartney, Hank Williams Jr., Bob Seger, the Thunderbirds, Cheap Trick, Elvis Costello, Joe Cocker, and George Benson. Dave is a member of the Songwriters Hall of Fame, the Rock and Roll Hall of Fame, and the Louisiana Music Hall of Fame. When Preservation Hall first began fifty years ago, Dave was forty. Lucky for New Orleans, Dave still picks up his trumpet every once in a while and graces audiences with his ageless power.

MARK BRAUD

Born in 1973 into the musical Brunious and Santiago families, Mark Braud didn't always know he himself would be a musician. "But I wanted to entertain," says Mark, "and I couldn't dance." When he was twelve years old, Mark's uncle Wendell Brunious gave Mark a cornet, and soon after that he met Walter Payton's son, Nicholas, in junior high school. Nicholas was already playing jazz, and this inspired Mark. "I had always listened to my uncles and my grandfather and thought: okay, this is music that older people play. But when I started meeting younger guys who were into music, it was an inspiration for me to play jazz and get more into listening to records." Mark says that even though he'd been listening to traditional jazz all his life, "I was listening to it from a different perspective then." Mark started his career with the Olympia Kids, an offshoot of the Olympia Brass Band for younger musicians, and soon went on to jobs recording, touring, and gigging with New Orleans legends of both traditional jazz and rhythm and blues, including the Tuxedo Jazz Band, Eddie Bo, Henry Butler, Harry Connick, Jr., and Dr. Michael White. Mark began playing at the Hall when he was thirty-four, and he says a lot of people comment on how young he is. "But at some point," says Mark, "all the other guys were young too. You don't start when you are sixty-five years old." Still, the talk around the Hall is that Mark has filled his uncle John Brunious' spot with the grace of a much older gentleman.

Ben Jaffe: I met Mark in high school. We both attended the New Orleans Center for Creative Arts in New Orleans. I was seventeen, Mark was fifteen. Mark had a head start on the other kids. His uncles, Wendell Brunious and the late John Brunious, were both leaders of the Preservation Hall band. Mark's grandfather, John "Pickey" Brunious Sr., was a renowned trumpeter, pianist, composer, and arranger in New Orleans. Mark recorded a wonderful tribute to his grandfather, "Hot Sausage Rag," a compilation of his grandfather's compositions.

KERRY BROWN

Kerry Brown grew up playing music in New Orleans' Baptist churches, and has been a professional drummer and musician for thirty-nine years. He began his professional career on the road with Clarence "Gatemouth" Brown, and has played with traditional New Orleans jazz legends Thomas Jefferson, Teddy Riley, the Amazing Ironing Board Sam, and Danny Barker, as well as with the Olympia, Excelsior, Tremé, and Royal brass bands and the Storyville Stompers. Kerry's vast musical repertoire includes playing and touring with blues musicians B.B. King, Freddie King, Albert King, Buddy Guy, Little Milton, Champion Jack Dupree, and John Mooney & Bluesiana. In terms of jazz, Kerry has played with the Jimmy McGriff and Hank Crawford Quartet as well as McCoy Tyner. Kerry has also played with the rock and roll icons the Allman Brothers and Jimmy Page, and the legendary country outlaw David Allan Coe. When he's not producing and directing the Gretna Heritage Festival (which he's been doing for fifteen years) or touring, Kerry can sometimes be found in New Orleans drumming at Preservation Hall.

JOHN BRUNIOUS

John Brunious was born into music. His father, trumpeter and pianist John "Pickey" Brunious, arranged songs for the likes of Count Basie and transcribed early jazz tunes for drummer Paul Barbarin. John "Pickey" schooled his son in traditional jazz as well. When John was nine and half years old, John "Pickey" took the family's only trumpet to a gig in New York, and while he was gone, John taught himself trumpet fingering using the Auburn method book and clothespins in place of valves. "Pickey" was impressed. John's musical education at St. Augustine High School included orchestral training, but as a young man John gravitated toward rhythm and blues and bebop, where he excelled at hitting the high notes. Following a combat tour in Vietnam, John recorded on sessions at Cosimo Matassa's J&M Studio, and he played bebop alongside Ellis Marsalis and drummer James Black. After substituting for Preservation Hall's trumpeter Percy Humphrey for several years, John joined the Hall's traveling band in the late 1980s, and went on to export his charm and charisma to audiences all over the world. John's rich voice and shock of white hair, along with his humor and warm heart, were some of his many trademarks that linger on today. In addition to his father, John's musical family includes his brother, trumpeter Wendell Brunious; his uncle, alto saxophonist Harold Dejan; and his nephew, trumpeter Mark Braud, who filled John's seat in the Hall's band after John passed in 2008.

DWAYNE BURNS

Trumpeter Dwayne Burns grew up surrounded by music in New Orleansí Sixth Ward, but it was when walking in the French Quarter with friends one day that he was struck by the sounds of trumpet aficionado Thomas Jefferson. Dwayne stood outside the club all day, listening. Dwayne officially began his musical career in elementary school, and went on to play in his school concert and marching bands. After graduating from St. Augustine High School, Dwayne became a regular in New Orleans' brass band scene, playing with groups like the New Birth, the Tremé, and the Doc Paulin brass bands, as well as traveling with the Olympia

Brass Band. Dwayne says he's addicted to music. He feeds the addiction, in part, by regularly blowing at Preservation Hall.

LESTER CALISTE

New Orleans native Lester Caliste played trombone in his St. Augustine High School band, and went on to study music at Xavier College. It was through one of Lester's teachers at Xavier that he met Allen Toussaint, and Lester went on to play trombone on many of Toussaint's recordings, including "Southern Nights." Lester played off and on at Preservation Hall and also with Harold Dejan's Olympia Brass Band, depending on his work schedule. Lester could sight read music charts, and when his day job became a night job, Lester turned from performing live to recording music with artists such as Johnny Adams, June Gardner, Reginald Koeller, and Patti LaBelle, whose massive 1975 hit "Lady Marmalade," produced by Allen Toussaint, features Lester on trombone. In the late 1980s, nineteen years after he stopped playing at Preservation Hall, Lester returned and played for fifteen more years. These days, Lester is retired and taking care of his elderly mother. We miss his kind and gentle soul.

MAYNARD CHATTERS AND MARK CHATTERS

As a young man, long before Maynard Chatters brought his trombone chops to the Hall's stage, he used to come by to listen to the Humphrey brothers after finishing a gig. Nowadays, Maynard can also hear his son Mark playing trumpet there. Sometimes, they even perform together!

Ben Jaffe: Maynard Chatters taught music at Dillard University for over thirty years. During his time there, he taught many of the musicians playing in and around New Orleans today. I came to know Mr. Chatters through his son Mark. Mark and I attended the New Orleans Center for Creative Arts together. Maynard comes from a large musical family: he has four brothers and eleven sisters. They all play music, and they all started out on violin. Recently, the Chatters family was honored with a family concert. It was beautiful to see everyone up on stage, from great-grand-children to great-grandparents. Besides being a great trombonist,

Mr. Chatters is a wonderful vocalist. I love it when he sings old spirituals.

FRANK DEMOND

Trombonist Frank Demond was born in 1933 in Los Angeles, California. Originally a banjoist, when he was in college, trombonist Big Jim Robinson persuaded Frank to switch to trombone as his main instrument. After moving to New Orleans in the mid 1960s, Frank played trombone in various parade bands as well as banjo with the Preservation Hall Jazz Band. In 1976, after Jim Robinson passed, Frank took over Jim's chair on trombone. Frank says he knew he was a permanent member of the band because "No one ever told me to go home!" In addition to playing in the Preservation Hall band, Frank ran his own record label, Smoky Mary Phonograph Company, which recorded Kid Thomas, Albert Burbank, Sweet Emma Barrett, and other giants. Franks says, "I must have played 'Just a Closer Walk with Thee' a thousand times before I went to New Orleans. But when you play it there with a brass band, at a graveyard, and there's a casket going down, it becomes a whole different experience. Going to New Orleans for the first time was like going from spring training with a high school team right to the Los Angeles Dodgers in the middle of a World Series."

Ben Jaffe says Frank grew up listening to recordings of early New Orleans jazz musicians. In his teens, he hung around The Beverly Caverns, a New Orleans jazz venue in Los Angeles. There he met his idols, clarinetist George Lewis, bassist Slow Drag Pavageau, and trombonist Big Jim Robinson. When banjoist George Guesnon took sick, George Lewis asked Frank to finish the run on banjo. Frank eventually moved to New Orleans to a house up the street from his mentor, Jim. To this day, Frank plays on Jim's horn. Frank began wearing his signature red socks in the 1980s as a tribute to Sweet Emma after her passing.

LARS EDEGRAN

Piano, guitar, and banjo player Lars Edegran was born in Stockholm, Sweden, in 1944. His father played guitar, banjo, and violin, and his brother also played piano. Lars studied for two years at the Juilliard School in New York and worked at a record company in Chicago, where he would go to blues clubs to hear musicians like Buddy Guy. In 1965, Lars moved to New Orleans, and on his first day in town, he went to Preservation Hall. Lars quickly became a regular at the Hall and began joining the musicians at house parties in the Tremé. Trumpet player Johnny Wiggs took Lars under his wing and got Lars work painting houses—including George Lewis's house. Lars has been greatly inspired and influenced by all the musicians at Preservation Hall and Dixieland Hall, especially banjoist Father Al Lewis and pianist Tuts Washington. Lars has recorded with numerous jazz greats, including Doc Cheatham, Sammy Price, Al Grey, Arvell Shaw, Danny Barker, Jabbo Smith, Al Casey, and Franz Jackson, as well as k.d. lang. Lars has toured all over the world playing music, including performances for the Queen of England with the cast of *One Mo' Time,* whose soundtrack was nominated for a Grammy Award, and at the Newport Jazz Festival, where he met Louis Armstrong and Mahalia Jackson. Lars's soundtrack for the movie *Pretty Baby* was nominated for an Academy Award. In 2010, Lars received an award from the Preservation Resource Center for outstanding musical contribution to the New Orleans community and jazz heritage. Lars has played at Preservation Hall off and on for the last forty years.

Ben Jaffe says Lars is one of a number of foreign musicians who moved to the city and became an important part of the music: "Growing up, Lars had a band called the 'New Orleans Ragtime Orchestra.' They would play written ragtime music from the early part of the twentieth century. They wore tuxedoes and played music I had only heard on record. Listening to them, I thought it sounded like being alive in New Orleans in 1910. When I joined the Preservation Hall Band in 1993, Lars was the pianist, along with Narvin Kimball on banjo. Between the two of them, I knew every night was going to be a new musical experience."

ERNIE ELLY
Ernest Anthony "Fat Daddy" Elly Sr., otherwise known as Ernie, was born in 1942 in New Orleans' Sixth Ward. His mother, Hilda Morris Elly, played violin. His brother, Frank Elly Jr., played drums and was Ernie's earliest teacher. Ernie's cousin Rudolph Peters played guitar, and his cousins Leonard and Melvin Morris still play trumpet and sing, respectively. Ernie wanted to play drums ever since he laid his eyes on them, and he's been doing just that for over fifty-two years. His band director at Joseph S. Clark High School, Evonne Bush, was a great influence, and after graduating, Ernie joined the Air Force. Ernie learned a lot of classics and standards in the Air Force band, but he wanted to play "some shake-your-booty music." Ernie got his chance with the Storyville Jazz Band, which included George and Bob French, Ellis Marsalis, Ralph Johnson, and Teddy Riley. "Boy, that was really fun!" recalls Ernie. "We used to play all kinds of different music. We'd play rhythm and blues, country and western, and traditional." Ernie loves drumming in a wide variety of genres. "I remember one day I played about four gigs and each gig was a different type of music. I was proud of that, you know," says Ernie. "A lot of times when people hear you or see you playing a certain kind of music, they figure that's it. They put you in a box." Music has brought Ernie around the world, including playing with Ray Charles at Carnegie Hall, the Apollo Theater, and London's Royal Festival Hall. Ernie has played with so many musicians he can't recall them all, but the list includes Jay McShann, Al Grey, Doc Cheatham, and the Dukes of Dixieland. Ernie has been playing in and out of Preservation Hall for over thirty years.

Ben Jaffe: Ernie has an individual, unique way of playing that is beyond description. He can stretch and bend time the same way jazz musicians and blues players extend and change the pitch of notes to make them sound more human. Ernie spent years on the road touring and recording with the likes of Sam Cooke and Ray Charles. His drumming is part parade beat, second line, traditional, funky, and modern all at once. There is this thing he does with the floor tom tom where he strikes the drum head repeatedly for dynamic effect. I've never seen or heard anything like his playing.

DANIEL FARROW
Daniel "Wennie" Farrow plays the whole saxophone family—

soprano, tenor, alto, and baritone. In 1945, when he was thirteen years old, he passed the room where the school band practiced and saw a lot of instruments and a lot of girls. The musical director asked Daniel what instrument he wanted to play, and Daniel replied he'd have to ask his mama—because during those days, you had to ask your mama. His mom told him to play the saxophone "because it's sweet" and from that day on, this idea of sweetness was instilled in Daniel. After a mere three months, Daniel played his first solo over the school's PA system. Daniel's grandfather played the guitar, his grandmother played the bass, and his grandfather's cousin, Papa John, played guitar at Preservation Hall. Daniel played in the Air Force band during the Korean War, and once he was back in New Orleans he started playing rock and roll in bars around town and in big bands for balls. Daniel played in second lines with the Tuxedo Brass Band and also with Kid Johnson, William Houston, Dave Bartholomew, the Original Crescent City Jazz Band, and Wardell Quezergue's Royal Dukes of Rhythm. In 1995, when Daniel wasn't playing much at all, he got his first call to play at Preservation Hall, where he's been a regular ever since. Daniel likes to close his eyes when he plays so he can hear the music better. He says playing at Preservation Hall makes him feel good about himself.

Ben Jaffe says Daniel is a true gentleman, soft-spoken with a sweet heart: "For many years, Daniel worked as a driver for a local department store. On the weekends and at night, Daniel would play for parades, dances, and at church on Sunday. To this day, Daniel still plays on the same horn he's had for over fifty-five years."

CHARLIE GABRIEL

Clarinetist, saxophonist, and flutist Charlie Gabriel is a fourth-generation jazz musician from New Orleans. Charlie's family came to New Orleans from Santo Domingo in the 1850s, and Charlie was born in 1932. His great-grandfather, Narcesse Gabriel, was a bassist who played opera, and Charlie's grandfather, accordionist and clarinetist Martin Joseph, played in his National Jazz Band with cornetist Freddie Keppard, as well as with blues singer Ma Rainey and reedman Sidney Bechet. Charlie began playing clarinet

professionally when he was eleven years old. It was during World War II, and musicians were in short supply. Charlie's father, Martin Manuel "Manny" Gabriel, was a clarinetist and drummer, and on the nights when he already had a gig and was asked to play another, Charlie's dad responded, "I'm working already. I'll send you the kid." Charlie was the kid. Charlie says he was raised by the musicians he played with in the Eureka Jazz Band—T-Boy Remy, Kid Humphrey, Kid Sheik, Kid Shots, Kid Clayton, and Kid Howard—who always brought him home in time for school the next day. "All my aunts, all my uncles, all my sisters, all my brothers, all my cousins—we all plays music. Everyone of us," says Charlie. Manny Gabriel taught music to his six sons and also at the school for the blind. "I use to like little girls," remembers Charlie, "and I'd try to catch up with them. My dad say, 'Son, if you play this horn—you chasing them little girls over there—they gonna chase you!' And that sure enough happened." Charlie has played with Tony Bennett, Frankie Avalon, Brenda Lee, Mary Wells, Eddie Willis, Joe Hunter, and many other early Motown artists. Charlie says, "I have many, many people inside of me that I have rubbed shoulders with, and I got something from each one of them. It's all wrapped up inside of me, and by me still playing today and still able to go around the universe, I give all these other things I have from those that I have came in contact with."

Ben Jaffe: I can vividly remember the day I first saw Charlie Gabriel. We were playing at a funeral procession. We didn't actually meet that first day. We marched alongside each other, the way I used to do with my godfather, Harold Dejan, noticing how much he reminded me of the older musicians I grew up with. There's a certain rhythm to the way older men walk in New Orleans. Charlie grew up in New Orleans in the 1940s. His family moved to Detroit where he spent over fifty years of his adult life, raised a family, and toured the world with the likes of Aretha Franklin.

JACQUES GAUTHE

French-born Jacques Gauthe began playing piano in 1944 at age five. He switched to clarinet when he was eleven. After hearing New Orleans' Sidney Bechet perform in Paris, Jacques officially began his career as a professional jazz musician. Jacques eventually moved to New Orleans to play music and cook, both of which bonded him to Allan Jaffe, one of Preservation Hall's founders. Jacques's sound on the clarinet was like him: robust and full of energy.

Ben Jaffe recalls one of the last conversations he had with Jacques, about making salami: "Once a year, Jacques would grind his own meat and hang it on a rope down the hallway to his back door. He told me he had to put newspaper down to soak up the oil from the drying meat. He said it was a lengthy and messy endeavor with delicious results. I asked how long it takes. With his typical shrug of the shoulder he replied with his heavy French accent, 'When it's ready. Until then, salami is my wife's enemy!' We burst out laughing." Jacques passed away in 2007.

JEFFREY HILLS

Tuba player Jeffrey Hills was born in New Orleans at Charity Hospital in 1975. His mother passed when he was twelve years old, but luckily, around the same time, Jeffrey started learning music in his school concert band, led by Dr. Herman Jones. Music showed Jeffrey a different way, and it became his passion in the midst of a difficult environment. Jeffrey's style, which he describes as "melodic like a trumpet player while still holding the bottom," has been greatly influenced by fellow sousaphone players Big Al Carson, of the Olympia Brass Band, and Kerwin James, of the Olympia Junior and New Birth brass bands, as well as New Orleans legends Tuba Fats and Edgar Smith, longtime members of the Olympia Brass Band. When he was only seventeen, Jeffrey began playing at Preservation Hall with the Olympia Brass Band, where he quickly became a favorite of not only the Hall's audiences, but the folks who work at the Hall. Jeffrey has played with nearly every brass band in the city, including the Dirty Dozen, Rebirth, Tremé, Lil Rascals, and New Birth brass bands, as well as the Jass Cats. Jeffrey has recorded with Ellis Marsalis, Leroy Jones, Mari Watanabe, and Russell Batiste, among others. Jeffrey is currently the lower brass instructor for Roots of Music, the free tutoring and music education program for New Orleans' youth.

Perhaps the highest praise for Jeffrey's musical chops comes from the many folks who say he is the one to fill the shoes of Tuba Fats. With his horn in his hands, Jeffrey looks downright angelic.

Ben Jaffe: We are fortunate to have musicians like Jeffrey Hills. He embodies what it means to be a New Orleans musician. Jeffrey got his early training in the Junior Olympia Brass Band, where he had the opportunity at a young age to play alongside veteran musicians like Harold Dejan and Milton Batiste. You can hear the spirit of New Orleans in every one of Jeffrey's big full round notes. Jeffrey still marches with bands at parades. Think about what it takes to carry and play a tuba for three hours. Now consider this, they are marching the entire time!

CAYETANO HINGLE

Bass drummer Cayetano Hingle grew up in New Orleans' Seventh Ward, and started playing the snare and bass drums when he was nine years old at Covert Elementary School. Tanio played in Harold DeJan and Milton Batiste's Junior Olympia Brass Band in the early 1990s, and went on to play in the Olympia Brass Band. These experiences, along with the styles of other traditional players such as Lionel Batiste and Benny Jones, strongly influenced Tanio's playing, which is a rich mixture of history with a funky, up-tempo style. Among the many bands Tanio has played with are the Bucketman, New Birth, and Magnificent Seventh brass bands. He recently recorded with Eric Clapton.

Ben Jaffe: When I was just starting out playing music, Tanio and I were band mates in the Tremé Allstars with James "Twelve" Andrews. On weekends and after school, we would play out on Jackson Square for tips. Tanio had the great fortune of knowing and learning from Noel "Papa" Glass, the bass drummer with the Olympia Brass Band. When Tanio plays, it sounds old and new at the same time. There's never a question where the beat is when Tanio's playing.

KERRY "FAT MAN" HUNTER

Kerry started playing snare drum when he was twelve years old in the Roots of Jazz Brass Band, led by Danny Barker. He went on to be the snare drummer for the Junior Olympia Brass Band in the early 1990s, where he got to know Harold Dejan and Milton Batiste. He later played in the Olympia Brass Band. Currently, "Fat Man" is the snare drummer for the New Birth Brass Band, but he plays snare for many others, including the Rebirth, Dirty Dozen, and Tornado brass bands. Kerry says: "A lot of stuff that we did as kids, what they taught us—the style of the traditional music, and how the music was played, and what music is the 'right' music and what music is 'not right' music—we still know it today. A lot of people who play brass band music is just thinking that you can just pick a horn up and play it because you was playing in the school band, but if you don't play this music for the feeling from your heart, it's not really going to be the New Orleans traditional brass band."

Ben Jaffe: "Fat Man" has such a relaxed, easy way about him. His playing is way beyond his years. He's fluent in early jazz to contemporary brass band. I wish I had half the soul Fat Man has in his left pinky. A lot of the rhythmic patterns you hear in New Orleans today came from Fat Man's snare drum. Growing up, we played together often in parades and on the street. He was one of the younger cats who really respected the older generation of musicians.

BEN JAFFE

Ben Jaffe was raised with Preservation Hall. He grew up two blocks away, and spent many of his evenings, weekends, and after-school hours there. Ben marched in his first Carnival parade at the age of nine alongside his father and Piran (godfather) Harold "Duke" Dejan. When he was thirteen, the lease on the building that housed the Hall was up for renewal. Ben's father, Allan Jaffe, who co-founded Preservation Hall along with Ben's mother Sandra, sat the family down and asked Ben whether they should continue. His parents felt they had accomplished their mission: to provide a performance space to the living New Orleans legends who created New Orleans jazz. Preservation Hall was a very modern concept in 1961. The civil rights amendments had not yet been passed, and New Orleans was a part of the Jim Crow

South. For whites and blacks to congregate socially and perform in mixed bands was strongly discouraged. But by 1984, much had changed. Many of the original musicians who had played at the Hall in its early days—George Lewis, Punch Miller, Billie and De De Pierce, Sweet Emma, Slow Drag Pavageau, Papa John Joseph, George Guesnon—had passed. Yet the soul of the Hall remained the same. Without question, Ben replied, "Of course you continue." Less than ten years later, the day after graduating from Oberlin College, Ben flew off to play upright bass with the Preservation Hall Jazz Band in France and began overseeing operations at the Hall in New Orleans. Ben returned to New Orleans with a renewed interest in perpetuating the musical traditions he grew up with.

Currently, Ben is the Hall's creative director, and he plays the tuba (sousaphone), upright bass, and banjo in the Preservation Hall Jazz Band. Ben remastered and released several archival recordings of the early Preservation Hall band, including recordings by Sweet Emma Barrett and Sister Gertrude Morgan as well as new recordings, including collaborations with the Blind boys of Alabama, Pete Seeger, Tom Waits, Trombone Shorty, Mos Def, Lenny Kravits, the Edge, and many others.

RALPH JOHNSON

Ralph Johnson started learning clarinet when he was seven from his father, clarinetist and alto saxophonist George "Son" Johnson, who made sure each of his eleven children prioritized practicing music over playing ball. Ralph described himself as a reed player, and though he is best known for his sound on clarinet and saxophone, he also loved playing the trumpet, piano, and flute. "If I take a trip with an oboe," Ralph said, "that's something else." Ralph played in the Imperial, Eureka, and Onward brass bands as well as in modern and traditional jazz ensembles such as Placide Adams' Dixieland Hall Jazz Band and Gregg Stafford and the Jazz Hounds. Ralph spent eight years playing rhythm and blues with Clarence "Frogman" Henry and ten years with soulman Jerry Butler. He recorded with Allen Toussaint and was in the horn section of Wardell Quezergue's band. Among many, many others, Ralph played with pianist Ellis Marsalis, saxophonist Nat Perilliat, trumpeter Wallace Davenport, and saxophonist Herman Sherman.

Ben Jaffe: Mr. Ralph and I played together for years. I got to know him real well. We used to call him "Sarge." I would always greet him by clicking my heels and saluting. He would always chuckle and salute back and then offer me both of his hands. When you spend as much time as we do on the road, you become family, —always looking out for one another. It was hard when Mr. Ralph's health began to fail and he couldn't tour anymore. He continued to perform at the Hall for years. The hurricane was hard on Ralph. He had a lot of family responsibilities. Ralph was not a man of many words, but when he did speak, pay attention. I remember talking to him about John Brunious. The two of them had known each other and played in the same bands together for over fifty years. He told me, "You know, John and I were REAL brothers . . . we didn't always get along." I've always felt it took a lot of insight and reflection to say something so profound.

RONELL JOHNSON

Born in 1976, Ronell Johnson began playing trumpet and piano when he was six years old under the guidance of his three older brothers, who are also professional musicians. When he was ten, Ronell began teaching himself to play the trombone, tuba, organ, saxophone, and drums. Ronell played at church, in school bands, and with his family band, Coolbone Brass Band. After studying music at the New Orleans Center for Creative Arts (NOCCA) and Southern University at New Orleans, Ronell went on to play with musicians such as Lars Edegran, Tommy Sancton, Michael White, Banu Gibson, Steve Pistorius, and the Paulin Brothers Band. Ronell's great-uncle, Joseph "Kid Twat" Butler, was the string bass player with the legendary Kid Thomas Valentine at Preservation Hall. With his regular appearances at the Hall, Ronell is carrying on the family tradition.

Ben Jaffe: When I taught in the jazz department of my alma mater, NOCCA, one of my students was Ronell Johnson. I can't take credit for Ronell. He was well on his way when we met. Ronell played in a band with his older brother Stephen "Coolbone" Johnson. They were a big deal. They took elements of hip hop and incorporated them into the traditional New Orleans brass band setting. It struck me as the same thing the old Olympia Brass Band did back in the 1970s when they started playing "I Got a Woman" and "Watermelon Man." Ronell is a beautiful person and amazing talent. It's heartwarming to know our tradition will live on in people like Ronell.

LEROY JONES

Trumpeter Leroy Jones was born in 1958 and taught himself to play guitar when he was eight years old. Leroy started playing cornet in grade school, at St. Leo the Great. As a member of the school's honor band, Leroy played the baritone horn, but the big case proved to be a bit of a burden during his mile walk to school. Leroy got his first trumpet in 1968. When he was twelve years old, Leroy's Seventh Ward neighbor, Danny Barker, heard him practicing trumpet in his garage and recruited him for the Fairview Baptist Church Band, which Leroy went on to lead. Sometimes, after finishing a gig in the French Quarter, Leroy and other members of the Fairview Band stopped by Preservation Hall to listen. Leroy went on to play in the Harry Connick Jr. Orchestra and become a member of the New Orleans Jazz Hall of Fame. Terence Blanchard remembers growing up in New Orleans around Leroy: "He was the guy that was well ahead of his time. He played with a command and maturity that is still unmatched. When I listened to him play I always imagined myself having that tone, or his sense of phrasing, and definitely his sense of rhythm. He was and still is my hero." These days, in between his world travels playing music, Leroy leads his own band at the Hall each week, where he delights audiences with his impeccable technique, his modern swing, and his warm, gentle voice.

REGINALD KOELLER

Trumpeter Reginald Koeller was born in Wilmington, Delaware, in 1921, but love and music eventually brought him to New Orleans. Reginald played with the Andrew Hall Society Brass Band, Harold Dejan's Olympia Brass Band, the Raymond Anchor Orchestra, Kendrick Johnson's Orchestra, and Andrew Morgan's Young

Tuxedo Brass Band. When the Audubon Park swimming pool was integrated in the late 1960s, Reginald played at the opening. Reginald loved J&B Scotch, but it never made him late for work with a range of musicians, including Dalton Rousseau, Herman Sherman, Lawrence Trotter, Tuba Fats, Grand Marshal Fats Houston, Emile Knox, Walter Payton, and his favorite trumpet player, Gregg Stafford. Reginald's last gig was a thirteen-year stint at Preservation Hall on Monday nights.

ANTHONY "TUBA FATS" LACEN

Known simply as Tuba Fats, Anthony "Tuba Fats" Lacen perhaps remains New Orleans' most renowned tuba player, seven years after his passing. Born in 1950 in uptown New Orleans, Tuba Fats grew up watching musicians and knew that was what he wanted to be. Sometimes, after his family was asleep, he would sneak off to the nearby Dew Drop Inn to hear Papa Celestin, B.B. King, and Bobby "Blue" Bland. He was big for his age and had hair on his chin, so he looked a bit older, but still, sometimes his mother caught him! Tuba Fats's neighborhood musical education included spending Sunday afternoons listening to bluesman Big Joe Turner. Before he was Tuba Fats, when Anthony wanted to play the trumpet, he cut a hose pipe, put a funnel on the end, and started blowing. By junior high he was playing brass band music on the street with the E. Gibson and Doc Paulin brass bands. When he was fourteen, Tuba Fats got in trouble with his band teacher for putting too much swing in the regular marches. Tuba Fats wanted to have the swing of a bass player, and this, along with turnarounds and his left-handed-reverse valve playing, made Tuba's sound distinct. For years, he led a band playing for tips in Jackson Square, where he encouraged and schooled countless younger musicians. Tuba Fats played with nearly every brass band in town, including the Young Tuxedo, Onward, Algiers, Tremé, and Olympia Brass Bands. Tuba Fats led his own band, Tuba Fats & the Chosen Few Brass Band, and he was one of the founding members of the Dirty Dozen Brass Band. Tuba Fats traveled around the globe playing music, and he made several jazz recordings on the Jazz Crusade label. Anthony "Tuba Fats" Lacen died in 2004. The second line for his jazz funeral, leading up to St. Louis Cemetery No. 1, packed the streets with beloved fans and musicians alike.

JOE LASTIE

Although the odds were always good that Joe Lastie would follow in the footsteps of his musical grandfathers, mother, aunt Betty, and uncles Melvin, David, and Poppee, his fate was sealed when Joe turned eight years old and received his first drum set. Joe played his first job in a rhythm section backing the Desire Community Choir, and along with classmates Wynton and Branford Marsalis, Joe studied jazz with Willie Metcalf at the Dryades Street YMCA. Joe took lessons from Clyde Harris in New York's public schools while his family briefly lived there. Back in New Orleans, on a tip from trumpeter Gregg Stafford, Joe was invited to substitute on drums at Preservation Hall in 1989. He has been a regular drummer with the band since then. "I come from the church," says Joe. "That's where a lot of my feelings come from. And when I was growing up in the church we would play the songs like we play at Preservation Hall."

Ben Jaffe concurs that Joe grew up surrounded by musicians: "Joe was born and raised in the Lower Ninth Ward around the corner from his grandparents. His family uprooted and moved to Long Island for Joe's high school years. Shortly after graduation and a stint in the show *One Mo' Time,* Joe moved back to New Orleans permanently. Joe's grandfather was a minister and is credited with introducing the drum set into church music. As a youngster, Joe would set up a small drum kit at the foot of his grandparents' bed and practice on whatever drums were available." "It didn't matter if it was just a snare drum and cymbal, I'd always find a way to make it work out."

CARL LEBLANC

After seeing the Beetles make girls scream on "The Ed Sullivan Show," Carl wanted a guitar. He played his first gig for money when he was twelve, and he's been a working musician ever since. Growing up, Carl drew musical inspiration from funk and jazz as well as rock and roll, and he received a musical education at Columbia University, Southern University in New Orleans, and, most importantly, from the musicians he played with—people like Fats Domino, Allen Toussaint, Screaming Jay Hawkins, Bo Diddley, and Ellis Marsalis. Carl's teacher at SUNO, Kid Jordan, played with Sun Ra in 1955, the year Carl was born, and he introduced Carl once he graduated. Sun Ra told Carl he didn't want anybody in the band who "knew" anything. He said: "I don't want nobody that 'know' because if you're playing what you know you're only dealing with a small slice of the pie." In recent years, Carl's musical evolution has turned increasingly on traditional New Orleans jazz. "How did I ever think I could play Charlie Parker and John Coltrane without first learning traditional jazz?" asks Carl. "That's like trying to do trigonometry before I learned arithmetic." When Carl was first called to sub on banjo at the Hall, he showed up with his hair in dreadlocks, his banjo set to guitar tuning, and, by his own admission, an attitude that didn't exactly inspire anyone to call him back. It took twenty years for a second chance to play at Preservation Hall, but by that time his hair was trimmed, the banjo tuned correctly, and his appreciation for tradition considerably deepened. Today, Carl regularly appears at Preservation Hall, a place he describes as very special. "It's like the spirit of the ancestors are here, and you can't deny it. Historically, the people that played here, the music that was played here, even down to the slave quarters in the back and the carriage-wait on the side for the horse and buggy. There's a lot of energy in here."

Ben Jaffe: To this day, Carl lives in the house he grew up in along St. Bernard Avenue, a major social thoroughfare where his family ran a small grocery/candy shop. Just up the street from his house is The Autocrat, an African American venue where traveling musicians like Lonely Teardrops, Ray Charles, and James Brown performed regularly. Carl remained a member of Sun Ra's Arkestra for eight years. In 1999, I took Carl uptown to Narvin Kimball's house. Narvin was a long-time member of the Pres Hall Band. Narvin, unable to perform due to a stroke, passed his banjo on to Carl. Carl is the director of the Preservation Hall music outreach program. Carl meets with students weekly to teach them the traditions and history of New Orleans music. "A lot of our cultural traditions are not documented. They are passed down from one generation to the next."

KERRY LEWIS
Ben Jaffe: I met Kerry back in high school. We were in the all-city jazz band together. Kerry attended St. Augustine High School, home to the Purple Knights and the Marching 100, the city's top high school marching band. Kerry was the first kid my age who had real "chops" on his instruments. It was amazing how easily he could get around the bass at such a young age. His natural sense of timing and rhythm were and are impeccable. He could hear something once and play it back with no problem. I started practicing a lot more after I met Kerry.

FREDDIE LONZO
When Frederick "Freddie" Lonzo's older brother was practicing on the horn their mother rented from Werlein's Music Store, he used to chase Freddie out of the room, and the horn became like a forbidden fruit. When Freddie was thirteen, his brother went away to college, and Freddie's mom wanted to return the horn. But Freddie told her to keep it. "I'll mess around on it," he said. Not long afterward, Freddie joined the school band, directed by Mercedes Stamp, and Freddie includes her as well as trumpeter Teddy Riley, tailgate trombone stylist Kid Ory, and trombonist Wendell Eugene—who blew his horn so loud that you could hear him two blocks away—as some of his big musical influences. But, says Freddie, "You learn something from everybody you've been around and seen and talked to. Good or bad, you learn something." When he was still a teenager, Freddie had his first professional gig marching in parades with EG Gabon and Doc Paulin's band. In college at Xavier University, Freddie played in rhythm and blues, rock and roll, and funk bands, including The Gladiators. Freddie's first big break was filling in with Paul Crawford's band, which led to playing with Bob French's Storyville Jazz Band. He also played in the Heritage Hall Band and the Olympia Brass Band. While working on Bourbon Street, Lonzo visited Preservation Hall to listen to players like Percy Humphrey, Kid Sheik, Alonzo Stewart, Manny

Crusto, Frank Field, and trombonist Waldren "Frog" Joseph. In the mid 1980s, Freddie began playing at the Hall with these older gentlemen, and now it is Freddie influencing younger musicians like trombonist Corey Henry. Freddie says, "The trombone is limited only by who's standing behind it."

Ben Jaffe has known Freddie for years: "Back when he was sixteen, he was in the Olympia Brass Band alongside my dad and Harold Dejan. Freddie's always had his own unique sound. His signature 'growl' can be heard across the river in Algiers! Freddie's got a great sense of humor. Freddie likes to joke, 'I am the sixth tenor, Frederrrrrrrico LLLLLLLonnnnnzo.' Joking aside, Freddie is an incredible talent and beautiful soul."

CLINT MAEDGEN
Born in 1969, reed player and vocalist Clint Maedgen grew up listening to his grandmother's jazz records. Though Clint was raised in a dozen different states, his mother and both of her parents were born in New Orleans. Clint's great-grandfather was a policeman in the French Quarter in the 1930s, and his Uncle Jack arrested Lee Harvey Oswald on Canal Street for handing out Communist propaganda. Clint attended high school in Lafayette, Louisiana, and studied clarinet with Alvin Batiste at Southern University in Baton Rouge before moving back to New Orleans as a young man. Before he began playing at the Hall, Clint was best known as a performer in the New Orleans Bingo! Show, as well as in the band Liquidrone. While on tour with the Preservation Hall Jazz Band, Clint spent hours at the piano with John Brunious practicing the nuances, phrasing, and note selection of traditional songs' melodies. He recently took up the Albert system clarinet—the same kind of horn played by George Lewis and Willie Humphrey.

Ben Jaffe: The first time I heard Clint perform was with the New Orleans Bingo! Show in the backroom of Fiorella's Café on Decatur Street. There were about fifty of us squeezed in there. It was hard to tell who was in the band and who was in the audience. Everyone was in costume. There was no stage, the band was set up on the floor the same as we do at the Hall. You could feel the power of Clint's voice, his passion and conviction. That single performance resonated deeply with me. It was the beginning of our relationship. Clint says: "It's important to me to be honest when I perform. To believe in the creation. You can't fake what these gentlemen do. This music's been running through their veins for generations. It's my job to honor it with the respect it's earned."

RICKIE MONIE
Pianist Rickie Monie was born in 1952 and raised in New Orleans' Ninth Ward. Both of Rickie's parents played piano in church, and at home they kept the turntable spinning records by Art Tatum, Oscar Peterson, Teddy Wilson, and other greats of gospel and jazz piano. When he was eight years old, Rickie's father informed Rickie he was going to play the piano too, and began teaching him. Later on, Rickie's mother sent him to a private instructor. "I wanted to go out and play football like the rest of the guys in the neighborhood," says Rickie, "but now that I've been all around the world, I'm glad my father chose my profession for me." Rickie came to know Milton Batiste, Manny Sayles, Harold "Duke" Dejan, and Sweet Emma "The Bell Gal" Barrett on trips he took with his family, and later by himself, to hear music in the Quarter. "Sweet Emma was a special person," says Rickie, "and she didn't like everybody. But you know she liked certain people, and we got along very well." In 1982, Rickie got his first call from Preservation Hall, to substitute for Sweet Emma after she suffered a stroke. To the delight of audiences around the world, he's stayed on board ever since. Among many others, Rickie has played with musicians Dave Bartholomew, Frogman Henry, Dr. Michael White, Gregg Stafford, and Topsy Chapman. After playing recitals as a piano student, Rickie always asked his mother how he did. "Well, son," she answered, "if nobody walks out, you're doing okay." These days, the traditional music Rickie plays at the Hall sounds a little different than it did when he first heard it, for it has the feelings of the musicians playing it today. But "nobody ever walks out," says Rickie, "so I think we must be doing something right."

Ben Jaffe: Both of Rickie's parents were amateur pianists, and Rickie grew up playing the piano and organ in church—something he still does today. After graduating from Dillard University, where he majored in woodwind instruments, Rickie joined the Olympia Brass Band and played alongside my godfather, Harold "Duke" Dejan. In the early 1980s, Rickie began coming by the Hall to sit in for the aging Sweet Emma Barrett. "The time I spent sitting next to Sweet Emma was like going back to school," says Rickie. "Words can't always communicate a musical idea or concept. Sometimes, you just have to be there and experience it for yourself."

LESLIE MUSCOTT

Born in England in 1941, Leslie Muscutt started playing banjo at the age of sixteen in various bands around London. He later toured with visiting U.S. musicians, such as Sonny Boy Williamson, Champion Jack Dupree, and Henry "Red" Allen. After moving to New Orleans, Leslie recorded with Kid Sheik, Pud Brown, Louis Cottrell, and many others, and he appears on the Grammy-winning CD *Doc Cheatham & Nicholas Payton.* Leslie first played at Preservation Hall in the 1970s.

WALTER PAYTON

Ben Jaffe: Walt's been a part of my life as long as I can remember. I started studying music with him at McDonogh 15 when I was in preschool. I wasn't supposed to be in band, but Walt knew my dad and he let me hang around. I went on to study upright bass with Walt. He lived on St. Philip Street at the time in Big Jim Robinson's old house right off Rampart, across from the park. I would carry my bass over to his house every Saturday morning. I didn't look forward to those lessons. He was hard on me. Extremely strict. He pushed me harder than any other teacher I've ever had. We would sit for hours playing scales up and down, a cigarette dangling from his lips. His salt-and-pepper beard. His rock-solid build. His stare. His playfulness. Walt was a great athlete. He studied karate for years and became a black belt. Walt was proud of karate and applied many of its lessons to life and music. I remember him staying up late at night, after our shows, practicing for hours. He made a bet one night that he could kick the sign hanging outside Preservation Hall, and the person he was betting eventually

backed down. I don't know if it was because the wage was too high or he actually thought Walt could do it! There was no doubt in my mind he could. . .

Walt taught school in New Orleans for decades. A mighty achievement. Hundreds, thousands of students passed through his classrooms. . . . He left behind a great legacy. His son Nicholas is one of the finest, most talented musicians I've ever known. I don't know a world without Walt. I miss his chuckle dearly.

MICHAEL PIERCE

When saxophonist and clarinetist Michael Pierce was in elementary school, John Philip Sousa marches were broadcast over the intercom system, and he fell in love with the sound of the obbligato parts on clarinet. As a young child, Michael studied under Clyde Kerr Sr. and Alvin Batiste. He went on to study the clarinet in high school, college, and as a graduate student at Juilliard, where he also studied classical music and modern jazz. In addition to the clarinet, Michael plays the entire saxophone family as well as the flute. Even longer than the list of instruments he plays is the list of musicians he's worked with: Frog Man Henry, Sullivan Dabney, Deacon John, Gregg Stafford, Lena Horne, the Temptations, the Spinners, Sammy Davis Jr., Stevie Wonder, and Aretha Franklin. Michael holds graduate degrees in music from Tulane, New Orleans, and Xavier universities, and he is currently a full-time professor at Southern University. Michael plays contemporary jazz with his own group, Cool Breeze, as well as gospel music with Shades of Praise, and he brings this vast repertoire to traditional music, venturing into modern and avant garde jazz idioms, be-bop licks inspired by Charlie Parker and John Coltrane, and classical references, while still staying in the traditional style. Michael's mother was a music lover who sang in the choir, and she encouraged Michael to study piano and play in church. Playing in the small personal space of Preservation Hall sometimes reminds Michael of church concert halls.

Ben Jaffe: I first met Mr. Pierce when I was in grammar school. Mr. Pierce, as I will always refer to him, was the substitute band teacher. I'm glad I've never had to be in those shoes. Our entire school was like one big gang. We used to get substitute teachers running in tears out the front door! Mr. Pierce was the exception. He talked slowly, with authority. He was the only substitute I ever remember returning to teach us on other occasions. As an adult, it's been a treat to get to know Mr. Pierce and perform with him.

STEVE PISTORIUS

Steve Pistorius was born in 1954 in New Orleans, and when he was growing up, his father brought home an old upright piano on the back of a pickup truck that he paid $25 for. The piano wouldn't fit in the house so it sat out in the carport, where Steve practiced melodies and chords. When Steve was eighteen, he answered an ad in the paper for a "barrelhouse piano player." This—Steve's first professional gig—ended up being at a Shakey's Pizza Parlor with banjoist Neil Unterseher, who gently scolded Steve on how to play with other people. To this day, Steve is grateful Neil didn't kick him out and get someone who already knew how to play! When he was in his twenties, Steve met fellow piano player John Royen, who shared his love for the older, traditional styles. Together they started playing at a venue in the Quarter called the Gazebo. At the time, Steve lived around the corner from the Hall, and Resa Lambert hired Steve to come by and sit next to Sweet Emma in her later years. When Sweet Emma was feeling too ill to play, Steve would take over, and Sweet Emma would pull on his shirt sleeve and tell him outrageous stories. Resa always insisted on playing Steve for a full night. While Steve was away on tour with Kid Sheik, Sweet Emma passed away, and Steve took over her seat. He was twenty-six. Steve's style is steeped in traditional music and has the rhythmic authority of one of his biggest influences, Jelly Roll Morton. In addition to taking the stage at Preservation Hall, Steve plays piano with Dr. Michael White and his Original Liberty Street Jazz Band as well as with his own bands, the Mahogany Hall Stompers and the Southern Syncopators. Steve says he has played on every steamboat in the world. He started on the Delta Queen in 1975, and he currently plays on the Natchez. Steve feels fortunate to have traveled the world playing music and meeting some of his heroes, like composer Eubie Blake and jazz and ragtime pianist Morten Gunnar Larsen—who has had a huge influence on Steve's playing.

Ben Jaffe: Steve has been playing around the Hall for years. He has a light touch that fits perfectly with the Hall's acoustic atmosphere. I've never known Steve to complain or be late. He's a wonderful stride piano player. I love listening to him play solo piano. I imagine people've been playing like him around New Orleans for over one hundred years.

MITCHELL PLAYER

Mitchell Player was nine years old when his music teacher in Shreveport, Louisiana, first showed him a string bass. It was love at first sight. Mitchell was a bit overwhelmed by the size of the instrument, but he knew it would set him apart from the other kids in the orchestra. Classically trained, Mitchell has played with symphony orchestras such as the Baton Rouge Symphony, the Mobile Symphony, and the Shreveport Symphony, but a passion for playing jazz eventually brought him to New Orleans. Mitchell plays in clubs and festivals all over New Orleans (and the world), but it was playing at Preservation Hall with Shannon Powell where he first learned how the music is supposed to *feel.*

SHANNON POWELL

Shannon Powell grew up in New Orleans' Faubourg Tremé, and by the time he was six years old, he was regularly playing drums for his church. When brass bands and second lines passed his family's home, Shannon was drawn to the drummers. Their syncopated beat and distinctive rhythms remain the root influences of Shannon's powerful, funky technique. Back when Shannon was still in elementary school, legendary stringman Danny Barker recruited him to play in the Fairview Baptist Brass Band, and Shannon went on to play professionally with Danny & His Original Jazz Hounds, starting at the wee age of fourteen. Shannon toured and recorded with fellow New Orleanian Harry Connick, Jr.; he also recorded with Ellis Marsalis, Jason Marsalis, Leroy Jones, Nicholas Payton, and Donald Harrison Jr. Among many others, Shannon has played with Diana Krall, Earl King, Dr. John, Marcus Roberts,

John Scofield, and Wynton Marsalis and the Lincoln Center Jazz Orchestra. Each week, Shannon delights Preservation Hall's audience by leading an inspired ensemble in which his drumming seems to bend time, creating space and dynamic energy. Shannon simultaneously highlights his fellow musicians and leads them to a place of feeling, as much as playing.

Ben Jaffe grew up a few blocks from Shannon: "We attended the same grammar school. My dad used to get Shannon's grandmother to bring him over by the Hall at night to listen to Cie Frazier, Louis Barbarin, Alonzo Stewart, and Freddie Kohlman. Just about everyday, you'd find Shannon over at Buster's, a local red-beans-and-rice joint that used to be on the corner of Burgundy and Orleans. By the time I graduated high school, Shannon was touring and recording with Harry Connick Jr. I remember the first time I saw Shannon at Madison Square Garden with Harry's big band and not believing my eyes. I was so proud of him."

THADDEUS RICHARD

Multi-instrumentalist Thaddeus Richard has music in the blood. Thaddeus's mother played the organ in church, and his father—bandleader, trumpeter, and composer Renald Richard—traveled with Ray Charles and wrote his breakout hit, "I Got a Woman." Other members of Thaddeus's large musical family include his cousins banjoist Don Vappie, bassist Richard Moten, clarinetist Dr. Michael White, bassist Richard Payne, and saxophonist Plas Johnson, who recorded with Frank Sinatra, Ella Fitzgerald, Sarah Vaughan, and Rod Stewart, among others. In 1969, Thaddeus cut his teeth on the Chitlin Circuit—the string of African American venues throughout the South and stretching all the way up to Chicago. On the Chitlin Circuit, Thaddeus was the bandleader for blues singer Z.Z. Hill, and he also played with Al Green, Joe Tex, Bobby Blue Band, Johnny Taylor, and Candy Staton. In 1974, Thaddeus moved to Nashville, Tennessee, and went to work for Buddy Killen at the SoundShop Studio, where he met Paul and Linda McCartney. Tommy Dorsey talked the McCartneys into listening to Thaddeus play saxophone on "Wild Prairie," an original composition by Paul. Thaddeus played a masterful solo,

and everyone started hollering. Afterwards, Linda shouted, "King Thaddeus!" Thaddeus spent the next five years working with Paul and still sees him from time to time. These days, part of Thaddeus's busy playing schedule includes regular appearances on piano at Preservation Hall. Thaddeus says his first love is God, but after God, it's music.

Ben Jaffe: Thaddeus is one of the most extraordinary musicians I know. He played sax and recorded with Paul McCartney's band, Wings. It was only in the 1990s that I learned what a talented pianist he is. Thaddeus loves all things food. He loves to cook, he loves to shop, he loves to eat. Thaddeus is also a great bassist and guitarist. I'm convinced if you locked Thaddeus in a room with any instrument, he could master it in no time.

JOHN ROYEN

John Royen was born in Washington, D.C., in 1955, where he grew up listening to his parents' jazz records. His father thought Sidney Bechet was the greatest, but it was Fats Waller who fed John's soul. He started playing music late in life, teaching himself ragtime piano when he was eighteen, and then taking lessons from John Eaton. John moved to New Orleans to finish college at Loyola University, but what he really sought was the city's connection to the old jazz music he loved. In fact, John spent so much time going out to hear music that he nearly flunked out of his first semester. "The amazing thing is that in New Orleans the music is an integral part of the culture," says John. "It's not something that is presented in a club from a band. It's a functional part of society. And that was a real revelation to me." John treasures the time he spent with the Humphrey brothers, Kid Thomas Valentine, Worthia "Showboy" Thomas, Kid Sheik, Ernie Cagnolatti, Narvin Kimball, and countless others who accepted him and performed with him. John's piano playing has also been influenced by Willie "The Lion" Smith and Jelly Roll Morton. Among many others, John has performed with Pete Fountain, Al Hirt, Jeff Healey, and Jack Maheu. John first started playing at Preservation Hall in 1979.

Ben Jaffe: I first got to know John back in the mid 1980s. I would carry my string bass down to the French Market or around the corner on Bourbon Street and sit in with him. John was extremely welcoming and always willing to take time to explain chord changes and show me different melodies. He was the first guy I ever knew to call out numbers instead of the name of the chord change, a little trick I use to this day. John studied with Don Ewell for many years. He plays in a stride style that is difficult to come by. John reminds me of the older men I grew up with. He's always impeccably dressed. He has the same style belt buckle I remember Jim Robinson used to wear.

TOM SANCTON

Author and clarinetist Tom Sancton grew up in two New Orleans worlds. During the day he went to school and played baseball in the milieu of a white middle class teenager—for some years, under segregation—but he also grew up inside another world: that of black New Orleans jazz musicians. At night and on the weekends, with his family, and later by himself, Tom went to the Hall to listen and learn, and to take music lessons with Punch Miller. Tom is a former student of the late, great George Lewis— an apprenticeship he lovingly chronicles in his memoir *Song for My Fathers.* Yet Tom says his passion for the world of musicians was about more than his love for New Orleans jazz music: "It was Sweet Emma, not just her music but the whole package you got with her—you know, the beanie and the bells. I mean, they were larger-than-life characters. There was an element of almost theater about it, too. You know, it was like a stage with these characters acting, playing music, but also talking and wandering around, and being something other than the type of people that I encountered in my other life." Tom credits his apprenticeship in and out of the Hall—which includes playing in parades with the Olympia Brass Band and eating red beans at Buster's—as a considerable factor in his acceptance to both Harvard University and Oxford University as a Rhodes scholar. In the years since he first sat in as a teenager at Preservation Hall, Tom has toured in Europe and the United States, been featured on more than a dozen CDs, and has played at major international jazz festivals, including numerous appearances at the New Orleans Jazz and Heritage Festival. In his "day job," he worked for twenty-two years as a writer, editor, and correspondent for *Time* magazine, including ten years as Paris bureau chief. Since his return to New Orleans, where he teaches creative writing at Tulane University, Sancton has played regularly at such legendary jazz venues as Palm Court, Snug Harbor, and of course, Preservation Hall.

JOHN "KID" SIMMONS

Trumpeter John "Kid" Simmons was born in London in 1943, where he grew up listening to jazz recordings. In 1964, he moved to New Orleans. John says, "When I first came here, the French Quarter was like a village. People who lived here in the French Quarter had never been on the other side of Canal Street in their lives." John spent most of his time at Preservation Hall listening to and playing with Punch Miller, Frog Joseph, Alvin Alcorn, Chester Jones, Joe Harris, Narvin and Jeanette Kimball, and many others. "It was the place to be if you were interested in New Orleans jazz," says John. "It was the only place to be." John worked at the Hall off and on for thirty years—selling records, collecting money, and introducing the band. At the Hall, John learned how to use his trumpet—to take time to express the phrasing of the instrument and the music.

Ben Jaffe says Simmons has been around the Hall since long before his time: "Simmons moved to New Orleans and married an African American lady, Dodie Smith Simmons. Dodie was one of the first employees at Preservation Hall. This is important, because when the Hall opened its doors in 1961, the civil rights laws had yet to pass. It was still illegal for blacks and whites to congregate in a social environment. Preservation Hall was at the center of the civil rights movement in New Orleans. The two of them lived around the corner from us over on Orleans Street, half a block from Buster's Restaurant. They lived above Bill Russell. I always looked up to the Simmonses for being so brave and for making a real difference."

DIMITRI SMITH

Sousaphonist Dmitri Smith started playing music when he was

eight years old. Classically trained on the tuba, Dmitri was in the all-state band and the all-American band, but it was as a member of the Olympia Brass Band that Dmitri learned the traditional New Orleans jazz songs that were sometimes as old as a century. Dmitri became hooked. "I never would have been able to imagine that I would stick with it, but no turning back now. I fell in love with it." In addition to regularly playing at Preservation Hall, Dmitiri leads the Smitty Dee Brass Band, founded to pass on to young musicians the traditional jazz styles and influences of New Orleans' famous musical predecessors—Louis Armstrong, King Oliver, Buddy Bolden, Bunk Johnson, and Jelly Roll Morton.

Ben Jaffe: The first time I remember meeting Dimitri was in the Rex Parade on Mardi Gras Day in 1987. My dad was sick and in the hospital. It had always been our tradition to march in the Rex parade together. That year, Dimitri took his place. I remember Dimitri being warm and welcoming. I learned a lot from him that day.

WILL SMITH
Will Smith grew up in Preservation Hall, where his sister Dodie Smith-Simmons worked, and his brother-in-law, trumpeter John "Kid" Simmons, sometimes played.

Will used to help push Sweet Emma's wheelchair to the car when her son came to pick her up, and most of the time she said something mean. "She was a real cantankerous old broad, but she was a great entertainer who captivated the audience." After following around his brother-in-law, Will couldn't wait to get an instrument of his own. His parents eventually bought him a trumpet, and it's been traditional New Orleans jazz ever since; Will's never wanted to play another genre. The musicians Will grew up with and who influenced him—people like Percy Humphrey, Ernie Cagnolatti, Kid Thomas Valentine, De De Pierce—remain a part of his musical fiber, and a part of his sound. In 1975, Will joined the Fairview Baptist Church Brass Band, led by legendary stringman Danny Barker, and he's played and toured with numerous traditional brass bands including the Storyville Stompers and Harold Dejan's Olympia Brass Band, as well as the "Doc" Pauline, Chosen Few, Tremé, Tornado, Lil Rascals, and Pinstripe brass bands.

Will is a little older than Ben Jaffe, and when they were growing up, Ben looked up to Will: "He was one of the few younger musicians to take an interest in older New Orleans music. We were playing at a funeral not too long ago and it felt like it did when I was little."

GREGG STAFFORD
Gregg's trumpet playing is steeped in tradition. Gregg was raised in a church, and though he's always been a very spiritual person, he never had a desire to become a musician. It happened by fate. After switching high schools, Gregg tried enrolling in an industrial arts class only to be told it was full. Luckily, the band leader was in the office when Gregg got the news, and after examining Gregg's mouth, he gave him a horn. Gregg wanted a tenor saxophone, but the band leader needed a trumpet player and handed him an old cornet. Nine months later, Gregg was promoted to the school band and started marching in parades. It felt good to wear a uniform and a band cap, and his mother always saw to it that his shoes were shined. Gregg was sixteen years old, and it was the late 1960s—the days of rock and roll—when brass band music was for "old men." But Gregg had grown up watching trumpet players play in brass bands, and he loved practicing the tunes at home. Gregg began playing in the E. Gibson Brass Band with childhood friends Tuba Fats and Michael Meyers and subsequently in Danny Barker's Fairview Baptist Church Band, along with a who's who of today's musical giants. Gregg also played in the Young Tuxedo Brass Band, which he went on to lead, and the Olympia Brass Band. Decades before he began regularly playing at Preservation Hall, Gregg started coming by to hear the music, but he absorbed much more from the musicians he thought of as fathers—Louis Cottrell, Harold Dejan, Albert Walters, Jack Willis, Teddy Riley, and many more. These men taught Gregg about history, pride, and values, and you can hear these elements in his hot, sweet, powerful, and tender style. Gregg says music holds the people and the community together; every time he plays, he holds audiences in rapture.

Ben Jaffe thinks Gregg Stafford is perhaps the best-dressed man in New Orleans: "His outfits are always impeccably tailored and well ironed, which matches his authentic old-time sound. His notes are pointy and stuttered. I love watching him sing. He is animated and full of spirit."

KATJA TOIVOLA

Katja Toivola got hooked on traditional New Orleans jazz while growing up in Finland. If she was awake fourteen hours of the day, she had the music on thirteen hours of the day. In 1995, she made her first pilgrimage to New Orleans and headed straight for Preservation Hall. These days, Toivola plays trombone at the Hall on a regular basis. Toivola also leads her own bands: the New Orleans Helsinki Connection and the Helsinki-based Spirit of New Orleans.

DON VAPPIE

Jazz banjoist Don Vappie has worked as a professional musician since 1971, but his family's musical roots date back to the late 1800s. During his early years, Don played rhythm and blues guitar and bass with several local New Orleans bands, as well as jazz guitar with the Dick Stabile Orchestra at the Fairmont Hotel's Blue Room, where he performed with the likes of Peggy Lee, Joel Grey, and Carol Channing. An equally accomplished arranger and vocalist, Vappie now leads his own ensembles, the Creole Jazz Serenaders and Don Vappie Quartet. Vappie records his own orchestral arrangements in which he performs as a banjo soloist, he appears as a regular guest with Wynton Marsalis's "Jazz at Lincoln Center," and he records and tours with a host of award-winning artists, including bluesman Otis Taylor and French Jazz Victory Award winner Patrick Artero. In addition to his work as performer and musical director in several documentaries and films, Vappie's work to conserve the Creole culture has earned him awards from the Louisiana Creole Research Association and the People's Award from the Creole Heritage Center. Vappie is a member of the New Orleans Jazz Orchestra and presently serves as the artistic director for the Cultural Alliance of the Americas.

MARI WATANABE

Pianist, composer, and arranger Mari Watanabe began piano lessons at age five in Tokyo, where she was born. She was a member of the New Orleans Jazz Club while attending Waseda University, and after her first visit to New Orleans, she decided to make it her permanent home. Mari has performed with local jazz legends such as Danny Barker, Dr. Michael White, Gregg Stafford, Ernie K-Doe, Tuba Fats, and Kermit Ruffins, as well as with Harold Dejan's Olympia Brass Band, the Dirty Dozen Brass Band, and the Chosen Few Jazz Band, which she now leads.

Ben Jaffe: Mari is soft-spoken and unassuming—that is, until she get's on the piano. That's when all language barriers are broken down. Once Mari moved to New Orleans from Japan, she immersed herself in the culture of the city. I remember her coming to the Hall to listen to Sadie Goodson and Jeanette Kimball. In New Orleans, it's always about the notes, it's about what takes place in between the notes. It's a challenging concept, one you won't find in any textbook. The only way to learn it is the way Mari did, go straight to the source.

ERNEST "DOC" WATSON

Doc was born in 1932, and when he was fourteen, he played in a trio known as "The Groovy Boys" with Ellis Marsalis and Roger Dickerson. Doc played French horn at Booker T. Washington High School, but he later turned to the saxophone, which he honed while serving as a staff sergeant in the U.S. Army during the Korean War. For thirty-five years, Doc played in the rhythm and blues group Lil Millet and the Creoles, and he also played in Herman Sherman's Young Tuxedo Brass Band and Harold Dejan's Olympia Brass Band. In his later years, Doc became a regular at Preservation Hall. Doc has traveled the world playing music. At home in New Orleans, he's influenced several generations of jazz musicians, including Benjamin Jaffe.

Ben Jaffe: Doc was in the Olympia Band with my father and Harold Dejan. Every Mardi Gras day, starting when I was nine, we would all gather uptown on Napoleon Avenue where the Rex parade lined up. After my father passed, Doc took me under his wing and would show me what to play during the different sections of the song. He was always jovial and excited to play. He loved to take photographs and toured the world with a camera strapped around his neck. Doc had this little dance he would do every night where he would stick his pointer fingers in the air and wiggle them like he was waving at someone. It was his signature dance. We always knew he was enjoying himself when he would do his dance. Ernest "Doc" Watson Jr. died in 2010.

CLIVE WILSON

Clive Wilson took up the trumpet after hearing the George Lewis New Orleans Jazz Band on tour in his native London. Clive studied physics at Newcastle University, but jazz was his passion, and after moving to New Orleans in 1964, he decided to make music, rather than physics, his career. When Clive first moved to New Orleans, he went to the Hall every night. At the end of the first week, the band told him to get his horn and sit in. A year later, Clive lived around the corner from the Hall with Lars Edegran. "Preservation Hall was our front room," says Clive. "We'd go down there at 8:30 or 9 and spend most of the night there, every night. This is before cell phones. It was before answer machines and things like that. You just went there and saw everyone you wanted to meet. It was like being in heaven for someone who wanted to be around this music and these musicians." Clive was soon playing in parades and jazz funerals with the Young Tuxedo, Olympia, and Eureka brass bands. During the 1960s he played second trumpet on tour with Billie and De De Pierce, and he later toured with clarinetist Herb Hall. Clive played with Freddie Kohlman's band, Papa French's Original Tuxedo Jazz Band, and along with pianist Butch Thompson, whom Clive met in Preservation Hall over forty years ago, he has produced programs for *The New Orleans Serenaders,* which revisits the classic repertoire of legendary New Orleans musicians such as Louis Armstrong and Kid Ory.

Growing up, Ben Jaffe remembers Clive always being on the scene: "I would sit in with Clive around the corner at Fritzel's or at the French Market. I learned a lot from Clive. He had a different repertoire than the other guys. Clive tended to lean towards what I thought were more obscure, often overlooked songs that had disappeared from the New Orleans songbook. Without Clive and many of the other Brits like Barry Martyn and Chris Burke, a lot of those songs would have vanished altogether."

Note: Information for several biographies was gleaned from the Preservation Hall Web site. *Keeping the Beat on the Street: The New Orleans Brass Band Renaissance,* by Mick Burns, was an invaluable reference for the biography of Tuba Fats and to a lesser degree Gregg Stafford.